Living Intelligence

The Convergence of AI, Biotechnology, and Advanced Sensors

Taylor Royce

DEDICATION

This book is devoted to the trailblazers, visionaries, and unrelenting information seekers. I hope that your love of invention and your steadfast dedication to breaking new ground will lead to a time where technology and people coexist peacefully for the benefit of all.

DISCLAIMER

This book contains information that is intended solely for educational and informational purposes. The information is not meant to be a replacement for expert consultation or as professional advice; rather, it is based on the author's research and understanding at the time of publishing. It is recommended that readers independently confirm any facts and seek advice from knowledgeable experts if they have any specific queries or worries about the topic.

No express or implied representations or warranties concerning the timeliness, accuracy, completeness, or dependability of the information provided herein are made by the author, publisher, or any related parties.

- It is entirely at your own responsibility to rely on any information in this book. Any direct, indirect, incidental, consequential, or punitive damages resulting from the use or reliance on this information will never be the responsibility of the author, publisher, or any associated businesses.
- The views presented in this book are those of the author alone and may not represent those of any institutions, organizations, or partners.

- For illustration purposes only, this book may contain references to outside resources, tools, or third-party content. The inclusion of any links or citations does not imply any association or responsibility for the content contained on external sites, and such references are given without recommendation or assurance of accuracy.

- The fields of science, technology, and regulations are always evolving. Any changes or upgrades that take place after publishing are not the responsibility of the author or publisher, and the content presented here represents the state of knowledge and technology at the time of writing.

- Because the various uses and possible hazards of convergent technologies might differ greatly depending on the situation, readers should use their own discretion and judgment while implementing any of the ideas or suggestions in this book.

By reading and using this book, you consent to absolve the publisher, author, and all other parties involved of any liability for any claims or losses resulting from your use of the information in it.

CONTENTS

ACKNOWLEDGMENTS.. 1

CHAPTER 1.. 1

Overview of Intelligent Life...1

    1.1 What is meant by "living intelligence"?............................. 1

    1.2 Convergent Technologies' Historical Development............... 4

    1.3 The Convergence's Driving Forces...................................... 7

    1.4 Living Intelligence:.. 10

CHAPTER 2.. 17

Foundations of Artificial Intelligence.....................................17

    2.1 How AI Technologies Have Changed................................. 17

    2.2 Neural Networks, Machine Learning, and Beyond.............21

    2.3 Advanced Algorithms and Cognitive Computing.................25

    2.4 AI's Challenges and Future Paths......................................28

CHAPTER 3.. 34

Biotechnology Developments...34

    3.1 The Modern Era of Biotechnology....................................34

    3.2 CRISPR and Genetic Engineering Technologies.................38

    3.3 Bioinformatics and Synthetic Biology............................... 41

    3.4 Biotechnological Advancements in Agriculture and Medicine
44

CHAPTER 4.. 49

Sensing Technologies at the Cutting Edge............................... 49

4.1 Sensors' Function in a Digital Environment........................49

4.2 Sensor networks and the Internet of Things........................52

4.3 Bioelectronic Interfaces and Biosensors............................. 55

4.4 Developments in Industrial and Environmental Sensing...... 57

CHAPTER 5.. 63

Convergence: Combining Biotechnology, AI, and Sensor Integration..63

5.1 Convergence Theoretical Framework................................. 63

5.2 Integrated Systems Case Studies.....................................66

5.3 Multimodal Intelligence and Data Fusion........................ 70

5.4 Overcoming Obstacles in Integration................................73

CHAPTER 6.. 79

Uses in Personalized Medicine and Healthcare........................ 79

6.1 AI-Powered Diagnosis and Therapy................................. 79

2. Improving the Planning of Treatment:................................ 81

6.2 Biosensors' Effect on Patient Monitoring...........................82

6.3 Genetic Profiling for Personalized Medicine........................ 86

6.4 Medical Ethical and Regulatory Considerations................... 89

CHAPTER 7.. 96

Environmental Monitoring and Smart Cities............................96

7.1 Sensor Integration and Urban Planning............................. 96

7.2 AI in Sustainability and Infrastructure Management.......... 100

7.3 Environmental Monitoring in Real Time............................ 103

7.4 Smart Cities: Policy, Privacy, and Security..........................106

CHAPTER 8..**113**

Education, Employment, and Social Consequences..................**113**

8.1 Using Adaptive Learning Systems to Transform Education.....
113

8.2 Training Employees in a Converged Technology
Environment.. 117

8.3 The Effects of Living Intelligence on Society....................121

8.4 Ethical Governance and Public Policy............................. 125

CHAPTER 9..**131**

Emerging Technologies and Future Trends............................**131**

9.1 AI and Cognitive Systems of the Future.......................... 131

9.2 The Prospects of Living Machines and Synthetic Biology. 135

9.3 Developments in Edge Computing and Sensor Fusion....... 139

9.4 Projecting the Upcoming Convergence Decade..................142

CHAPTER 10..**151**

Difficulties, Hazards, and Management..................................**151**

10.1 Privacy and Ethical Issues in Living Intelligence............ 152

10.2 The Dangers of Technological Disruption and
Overdependence.. 155

10.3 Governance Models and Regulatory Frameworks............ 158

10.4 Mitigation and Responsible Innovation Techniques......... 161

ABOUT THE AUTHOR..**169**

ACKNOWLEDGMENTS

My heartfelt appreciation goes out to everyone who helped to make this book possible. I want to express my gratitude to my family and friends for their continuous understanding, support, and encouragement along this journey. You have always been a source of strength because you believe in my goal.

I am really appreciative of the mentors, coworkers, and specialists in biotechnology, sensor technologies, and artificial intelligence who so kindly contributed their knowledge and experience. In addition to improving the book's substance, your contributions have motivated me to advance multidisciplinary innovation.

I want to express my sincere gratitude to the academic and research communities whose innovative work and unwavering curiosity are still influencing technology today. The concepts discussed in these pages are based on your discoveries and breakthroughs.

I would especially like to thank my publisher, editor, and

the full production crew for their crucial help and direction in making this project a reality. This work has been refined and presented thanks in large part to your devotion to quality and perfection.

Finally, I want to express my gratitude to the readers as well as the larger community of intellectuals and innovators who encourage the continuous search for knowledge. May this book act as a spark for additional research and discussion, advancing knowledge and understanding in a rapidly changing technological environment.

CHAPTER 1

OVERVIEW OF INTELLIGENT LIFE

In this first chapter, we offer the idea of Living Intelligence, a revolutionary concept that embodies the fusion of biotechnology, advanced sensor technology, and artificial intelligence. Similar to living things, living intelligence refers to systems that are able to learn, adapt, and change over time in addition to carrying out duties. By defining the idea, describing its historical development, examining the dynamics that led to its convergence, and summarizing the enormous potential and influence it has for many industries, this chapter establishes the foundation.

1.1 What is meant by "living intelligence"?

A new concept known as "living intelligence" combines the traditionally separate domains of biotechnology, sensor technology, and artificial intelligence (AI) to produce dynamic, adaptable systems. We must first outline this concept's constituent parts and the special benefits that come from combining them in order to completely comprehend it.

Discipline Integration: Living Intelligence is more than the sum of its parts. It symbolizes a complex weaving together of:

- Algorithms and machine learning models that analyze data, spot trends, and make decisions on their own are examples of artificial intelligence.
- The use of biological systems and species, including genetic and molecular technologies, to create innovative solutions is known as biotechnology.
- Sensor Technology: Sophisticated sensors that gather and transmit data in real time from the physical world.

The following important terms need to be specified in order to provide a clear foundation:

1. **Adaptive Systems:** These are systems that can change how they behave in response to experiences and incoming data. Adaptation is dynamic and ongoing in living intelligence.
2. **Evolutionary Learning:** Under Living Intelligence

frameworks, systems have the capacity to evolve improving their performance over time through iterative learning processes in contrast to static algorithms.

3. **Convergence:** This is the moment when biotechnology, sensor technology, and artificial intelligence (AI) all intersect and work together to create new, emergent capabilities that go beyond the constraints of each discipline alone.

The "Living" systems' scope:

In Living Intelligence, the word "living" emphasizes the notion that these systems have traits similar to those of biological beings. They are intended to:

- Learn from prior experiences and environmental inputs.
- Real-time adaptation to changes.
- Without direct human interaction, they may potentially improve their operating models and incorporate fresh data.

A new era of technical innovation is ushered in by this convergence, one in which systems are proactive rather than reactive, always improving to meet novel difficulties.

1.2 Convergent Technologies' Historical Development

The idea of convergence has a long history. Understanding the beginnings of the three convergent domains and how their past advancements have prepared the ground for this creative fusion is essential to appreciating Living Intelligence.

1. The first step is to trace the origins:

Artificial Intelligence:
- The idea of machines that could mimic human intelligence was first put forth by pioneers like Alan Turing in the middle of the 20th century, when artificial intelligence (AI) was still a speculative concept. AI has changed dramatically throughout the years, moving from rule-based systems to the introduction of neural networks. The creation of machine learning algorithms in the 1980s is one of the major innovations.
- Large data sets and more processing power propelled

deep learning's ascent in the early 2010s.

The field of biotechnology

- The origins of biotechnology can be traced back to ancient methods such as selective breeding and fermentation. However, the development of recombinant DNA technologies and, more recently, gene-editing methods like CRISPR marked the beginning of contemporary biotechnology in the late 20th century. Our capacity to modify biological systems at the molecular level has been completely transformed by these developments.

This is the sensor technology:

- Since the industrial revolution, sensors have played a crucial role in scientific advancement. Sensors were the first crude instruments for determining humidity, pressure, or temperature. Rapid developments in wireless communication, microelectronics, and materials research over the past few decades have produced extremely complex sensor networks that can continuously and in real time collect data.

2. Milestones that Paved the Way for Convergence:

- The development of digital computing gave rise to a

platform for enhanced data processing and artificial intelligence.

- Significant developments in biotechnology included the Human Genome Project, which established the groundwork for genetic engineering and personalized medicine.

- As the Internet of Things (IoT) grew, sensors from many settings were connected and became essential parts of intelligent systems. These sensor networks and big data analytics together made it possible to efficiently comprehend and use enormous amounts of data, bridging the gap between the collection of raw data and wise decision-making.

3. Initial Trials and Pioneering Moments:

- Early AI tests showed that robots could mimic human decision-making in a few specific fields, such as the creation of expert systems in the 1970s and 1980s.

- The discovery of CRISPR in 2012 revolutionized the field of biotechnology by providing previously unachievable levels of gene editing precision.

- Health monitoring systems that could continually

track vital signs emerged as a result of sensor technology advancements brought about by the 2010s wearable and mobile device boom.

These past advancements have prepared the way for the present day, when combining biotechnology, sensor technology, and artificial intelligence is not only feasible but also becoming more and more necessary to address difficult, real-world problems.

1.3 The Convergence's Driving Forces

The integration of these cutting-edge technology is driven by a number of forces coming together. To understand why Living Intelligence is becoming a transformative force, it is essential to comprehend these drivers.

1. Financial Aspects:

Market Forces:
Businesses need to innovate quickly in the current competitive environment in order to hold onto their market positions. Businesses may increase productivity, save

operating expenses, and create novel products by combining AI, biotech, and sensor technologies.

Trends in Funding:

Research and development has been driven by large investments from the public and commercial sectors. Government programs around the world are offering grants and subsidies for innovation in these disciplines, and venture capital funding for AI and biotech firms has increased dramatically.

Cost Savings and Efficiency Improvements:

Automation and better resource management made possible by converged technology can result in significant cost savings across a range of sectors, including manufacturing and healthcare.

2. Technological and Social Aspects:

Digital Transformation:

Almost every element of society has changed as a result of the current digital revolution. Digital technologies are being used by both governments and businesses to boost growth, improve services, and improve people's quality of life. A continuation of this approach that pushes the limits of what is possible is living intelligence.

The concept of globalization

Because of the interconnectedness of the world economy, technical advancements are quickly disseminated internationally. Collaboration and convergence become essential tactics for gaining a competitive edge as nations vie to be leaders in cutting-edge technologies.

Consumption Demand:

Consumers of today demand dependable, effective, and customized goods. Through smart home appliances or personalized medicine, the convergence of these technologies promises solutions that meet the demands of each individual.

3. Policy Initiatives and Regulatory Support:

- Governments everywhere are establishing policies to encourage the development of emerging technologies as they realize their strategic significance. These consist of tax breaks, funding for research, and legal structures intended to promote creativity while maintaining morality and safety.

- The development and implementation of integrated systems are further accelerated by investments in digital infrastructure and programs encouraging technological convergence.

When combined, these forces produce a strong environment that fosters the development of living intelligence, where societal demands, economic imperatives, and supportive legislative frameworks work together to push the limits of technological capabilities.

1.4 Living Intelligence:

1. Its Promise and Effect

The potential of living intelligence is enormous in many different fields. AI, biotechnology, and sensor technologies are coming together to change industries, boost productivity, and improve people's quality of life. This section examines the potential uses, advantages, and new difficulties associated with this game-changing technology.

Personalized treatment, real-time monitoring, and predictive diagnostics are just a few of the ways that living intelligence has the potential to transform patient care across all industries. Imagine wearable technology that can anticipate possible health problems before they become serious in addition to monitoring vital indicators.

Bullet Points:

- Biosensors are used for ongoing monitoring.
- Early disease identification using predictive analytics.
- Personalized therapy regimens based on real-time and genetic data.

Smart Cities: AI and integrated sensor networks can optimize urban infrastructure, boosting public safety, lowering energy use, and managing traffic.

Bullet Points:

- Monitoring of the environment in real time.
- Allocating resources intelligently.
- Improved emergency response and public services.

Industrial Automation: Convergent technologies, such as autonomous robots and predictive maintenance systems, allow for more intelligent industrial processes, lowering downtime and boosting output.

Education:

Living Intelligence-powered adaptive learning systems can customize learning experiences by adjusting lesson plans and instructional strategies to meet the needs of each unique student.

2. Expected Advantages:

Efficacy:

Living Intelligence has the potential to significantly increase production and service delivery efficiency by automating intricate procedures and optimizing resource utilization. Better performance and reduced operating expenses result from this.

Personalization:

Highly customized solutions are made possible by the

combination of biotechnology and artificial intelligence. This could include learning experiences that adjust to a student's progress and learning preferences in education, as well as therapies in healthcare that are customized based on a person's genetic composition.

The concept of sustainability

Smarter environmental management, waste reduction, and energy optimization are all made possible by intelligent systems. These solutions can assist sustainable growth and lower carbon footprints in sectors like industry and urban planning.

3. New Questions in Ethics, Regulation, and Society:

Ethical Aspects to Take into Account:

tremendous power with a tremendous deal of responsibility. Living systems' capacity for learning, adaptation, and evolution presents moral dilemmas pertaining to accountability, control, and autonomy. To what extent should machines be allowed to make decisions? What ethical ramifications result from systems that are capable of developing without direct human involvement?

Regulatory Structures:

The current regulatory frameworks might not be sufficient as these technologies merge. To handle concerns about data security, privacy, and the secure implementation of autonomous systems, new guidelines and regulations will be required. In order to safeguard the public interest and prevent innovation from being repressed, policymakers must collaborate with industry professionals.

The societal impact:

Significant societal changes could result from the broad adoption of living intelligence. Although there are numerous advantages to greater efficiency and personalization, there is also a chance that jobs may be lost and inequality will rise. Education, retraining, and careful policy preparation are all necessary to get society ready for these changes.

In conclusion, Living Intelligence has the potential to completely change the way we use technology. We are seeing the emergence of dynamic, adaptive, and strikingly lifelike systems by fusing the computing power of artificial intelligence (AI) with the accuracy of biotechnology and the real-time data capacities of sophisticated sensors. By describing the idea, going over its historical development, examining the factors that led to its convergence, and examining its enormous potential and influence, this chapter has established a thorough basis.

From the promise of building smarter, more sustainable cities to the ability to save lives through tailored treatment, the ramifications of living intelligence are extensive and far-reaching. However, these potential also bring with them difficulties that call for strong moral standards, flexible legal systems, and proactive social planning. We will explore each of these topics in further detail as we go through this book, offering a thorough road map of how Living Intelligence is influencing business, society, and technology in the future.

In addition to focusing on technological developments, this exploration of the intersection of AI, biology, and sensor technologies aims to redefine what intelligence actually is in the contemporary world. By empowering people, redefining the lines between the digital and biological realms, and transforming industries, living intelligence holds the potential to usher in a period of unparalleled creativity and human advancement.

CHAPTER 2

Foundations of Artificial Intelligence

This chapter explores the fundamental components that make up artificial intelligence. It looks at the fundamentals of machine learning and neural networks, analyzes the development of AI technologies from their infancy to the current deep learning period, and talks about cognitive computing and newly developed adaptive algorithms. Lastly, it describes the difficulties that present AI technologies confront and provides information about potential future paths that could result in more human-centered systems.

2.1 How AI Technologies Have Changed

There have been significant changes in both theory and application throughout the development of artificial intelligence. Gaining an understanding of this development is crucial to understanding how AI has developed from basic rule-based systems to the complex deep learning models that now lead the field.

Initial Rule-Based Frameworks:

Rule-based systems were the hallmark of AI in its early phases. These systems were made to carry out tasks by according to preset "if-then" rules or sets of instructions. Early initiatives such as the 1960s chatbot ELIZA demonstrated the potential of utilizing pre-written responses to mimic human speech. These systems established the foundation for more sophisticated thinking processes, notwithstanding their limited capacity for adaptation.

Important discoveries and advancements in algorithms:

A number of significant discoveries interspersed the transition from rule-based systems to more dynamic models:

- **Expert Systems:** Expert systems first appeared in the 1970s and 1980s. To address particular issues, like diagnosing illnesses or repairing industrial machinery, these systems made use of a knowledge foundation of rules that were developed by human professionals.

- The human brain served as the inspiration for neural networks, which gained popularity in the 1980s. These networks were initially straightforward and had trouble with problems like the vanishing gradient problem. They did, however, signify a change away from strict norms and toward learning from data.

- **Deep Learning Revolution:** Deep learning, a branch of machine learning that uses multi-layered neural networks to evaluate enormous volumes of data, was the true breakthrough in the 2010s. AI was transformed by breakthroughs like recurrent neural networks (RNNs) for sequential data and convolutional neural networks (CNNs) for image processing. With additional data and processing power, these models could learn hierarchical representations and perform better.

- Alongside architectural advancements, algorithms like backpropagation, dropout, and optimization techniques like Adam and RMSProp were essential in improving learning effectiveness and reducing overfitting.

The effect of computational power is as follows:

Deep learning research has accelerated due in large part to the enormous growth in computer capacity, especially through GPUs and specialized hardware like TPUs (Tensor Processing Units). Researchers were able to convert theoretical discoveries into useful applications by training larger, more intricate models thanks to this increased processing capacity.

Big Data Integration:

Modern AI has been fueled by the proliferation of digital data from social media, the Internet, and sensor networks. Deep learning models have achieved impressive accuracy in tasks ranging from natural language processing to picture and speech identification thanks to their capacity to process and learn from petabytes of data.

In conclusion, the development of AI has moved from rule-based, manually coded systems to complex, data-driven deep learning structures. Because of advancements in algorithms, computing power, and the accessibility of massive datasets, each stage of this evolution has built on the one before it.

2.2 Neural Networks, Machine Learning, and Beyond

Machine learning, which enables computers to learn from data and make judgments without explicit programming, is at the core of contemporary artificial intelligence. The foundations of machine learning, the function of neural networks, and the several learning paradigms that have been developed are all covered in this part.

The foundations of machine learning are as follows:

A branch of artificial intelligence called machine learning (ML) is concerned with creating algorithms that can recognize patterns in data and get better over time. Machine learning (ML) systems are made to recognize patterns and provide predictions using statistical inference rather than rigidly following instructions.

Essential Elements:

- **Data:** The fundamental component, since algorithms are trained on previous data.
- The quantifiable qualities or traits of the data that the

algorithm utilizes to learn are known as features.

- **Models**: mathematical frameworks that represent the connections among the data.

- The act of modifying model parameters to reduce error and increase accuracy is known as "training."

The function of neural architectures

A type of machine learning model called a neural network is based on the architecture of the human brain. They are made up of layers of interconnected nodes, or neurons, that process information collectively.

Important Types of Neural Networks:

1. The most basic type, known as a feedforward neural network, transfers data from input to output in a single direction.

2. Convolutional layers are used by Convolutional Neural Networks (CNNs), which are mainly designed for image data, to automatically and adaptively learn spatial hierarchies of information.

3. Recurrent Neural Networks (RNNs): These networks retain a type of memory to capture temporal dependencies, making them appropriate for

sequential data, such as text or time series.

4. Generative Adversarial Networks (GANs): GANs are used to create new data samples that replicate a specified distribution. They are composed of a discriminator and a generator.

Machine Learning Learning Paradigms:

Based on the kind of feedback given during training, machine learning techniques can be roughly divided into the following categories:

1. Learning Under Supervision:

Description: entails using labeled datasets to train models, with an output label assigned to each training example.

- Regression problems, spam detection, and image categorization are a few examples.
- **Methods:** Deep neural networks, support vector machines (SVMs), and decision trees.

2. Learning Without Supervision:

In order to find hidden patterns or inherent structures, the model is trained on data that does not have explicit labels.

- **Instances:** dimensionality reduction, anomaly

detection, and clustering.

- **Techniques:** Principal component analysis (PCA), autoencoders, and K-means clustering.

3. Learning Reinforcement:

By interacting with an environment and earning rewards or penalties, an agent gains decision-making skills.

- Autonomous vehicles, robotics, and gaming (like AlphaGo) are a few examples.

The following techniques are used:

- deep reinforcement learning, policy gradients, and Q-learning.

In addition to conventional neural networks:

The area is investigating increasingly flexible, adaptable models as research progresses, going beyond traditional neural networks:

- Reducing training time and improving performance by applying previously taught models to new, related problems is known as "transfer learning."
- **Meta-Learning:** Also referred to as "learning to learn," this method concentrates on models that can swiftly adjust to novel tasks using little data
- Self-supervised learning is a paradigm that lessens

the need for manually labeled datasets by allowing models to create their own labels from the data.

The foundation of contemporary AI is made up of these strategies and tactics. They offer the resources required to develop models that can carry out difficult tasks with greater autonomy and precision as well as to glean valuable insights from data.

2.3 Advanced Algorithms and Cognitive Computing

The goal of cognitive computing is to use computer systems to simulate human decision-making and mental processes. Cognitive computing seeks to mimic human cognitive processes including reasoning, perception, and problem-solving, in contrast to traditional AI, which frequently works in a limited field.

An Overview of Cognitive Computing:

Systems that use cognitive computing are made to communicate with people in normal language, comprehend context, and offer insights that go beyond simple data processing. In order to interpret unstructured data, learn from interactions, and adjust to new information, these systems incorporate a variety of AI approaches.

The following are core characteristics:

- Machines can comprehend and produce human language thanks to natural language processing, or NLP.
- Similar to human cognition, contextual reasoning is the capacity to understand information in its context.
- Learning and Adaptation: Iterative learning procedures that promote continuous progress.

The Potential of Up-and-Coming Algorithms:

At the forefront of enabling self-improving and adaptable systems are sophisticated algorithms:

- Natural selection serves as the inspiration for evolutionary algorithms, which iteratively choose, alter, and recombine potential solutions in order to progress toward the best outcomes.
- **Bayesian Methods:** Offer frameworks for probabilistic reasoning to assist control uncertainty in judgment.
- In order to build systems that can learn from both

large volumes of data and interactions with their surroundings, hybrid models combine various learning paradigms, such as deep learning and reinforcement learning.

Cognitive Computing Applications:

Applications for cognitive computing systems are numerous and span several industries:

- **Healthcare:** Supporting patient care management, individualized treatment programs, and diagnostics.
- **Finance:** Improving risk management, algorithmic trading, and fraud detection by interpreting data more effectively.
- **Customer Service:** Enhancing virtual assistant and chatbot interactions to deliver more contextually appropriate and human-like responses.

Difficulties in Copying Human Thought:

Cognitive computing still has a lot of obstacles to overcome despite its remarkable advancements. These consist of:

- The intricacy of human cognition is such that it is very challenging to fully recreate in a machine since human thought is so complex and context-dependent.

- **Integration of Diverse Data Sources:** Cognitive systems need to combine both organized and unstructured data, which calls for a lot of processing capacity and complex algorithms.

- **Scalability and Real-Time Processing:** One of the biggest challenges is still processing large volumes of data with real-time responsiveness.

A crucial area of artificial intelligence is represented by cognitive computing, which takes a comprehensive approach to simulating human intelligence. By overcoming the drawbacks of conventional algorithmic techniques, it aims to create increasingly efficient and natural reasoning, learning, and interaction systems.

2.4 AI's Challenges and Future Paths

Even though AI has advanced remarkably, a number of issues still exist that prevent it from reaching its full potential. In order to direct future research and innovation, it is essential to comprehend these constraints.

Restrictions and Difficulties:

The concept of bias and fairness

AI programs are only as good as the training data. Data bias can produce unfair and discriminating results.

Bullet Points:

- Historical inequities may be reflected in training data.
- Inadvertent bias in algorithm design has the potential to sustain unjust behaviors.

Comprehensibility:

- Complicated deep learning models, sometimes called "black boxes," make it challenging to comprehend the decision-making process.
- Regulatory compliance, accountability, and trust are all hampered by this lack of openness.

The computation cost is as follows:

- State-of-the-art model training necessitates extensive computational resources, which raises expenses and energy consumption.

- This can hinder innovation in smaller businesses and restrict access to only well-funded groups.

Predicting Future Patterns:

Edge AI:

- Lower latency, more privacy, and less bandwidth consumption are all promised when AI computation is moved from centralized data centers to edge devices.
- Real-time decision-making in applications like smart sensors and driverless cars may be made possible by this decentralization.

This includes quantum-enhanced algorithms:

- By resolving intricate optimization and pattern recognition issues that are beyond the capabilities of traditional computers, quantum computing has the potential to completely transform artificial intelligence.
- Although they are still in their infancy, quantum-enhanced algorithms have the potential to significantly increase model accuracy and speed up

learning.

A Pathway to AI That Is More Human-Centric:

The importance of explainability:

- Transparency must be considered in the design of future AI systems. Creating techniques for model interpretability is crucial to fostering trust and enabling cooperation between humans and AI.

- Research is now being conducted on methods like interpretable neural networks and model-agnostic explanation tools.

Governance and Ethical Frameworks:

- To solve issues with privacy, justice, and accountability, it will be essential to establish strong ethical standards and legal frameworks.

- Policymakers, academia, and industry working together can guarantee that AI development is consistent with social ideals.

Adaptive and Inclusive Education:

- AI needs to be more inclusive by embracing a variety of data sources and being cognizant of contextual and cultural differences.

- Like human learning processes, future systems should be able to learn throughout their lives and continuously adapt as new information becomes available.

Reducing the Impact on the Environment:

- Because AI still has a high computational cost, it is crucial to conduct research on energy-efficient hardware and algorithms.
- Hardware optimization and green computing innovations can lessen AI's negative environmental effects.

In conclusion, even if artificial intelligence has advanced significantly in recent decades, there are still many obstacles in the way that need to be carefully overcome. Although bias, interpretability, and processing costs are significant obstacles, they also present chances for additional innovation. AI may become more effective, transparent, and consistent with human ideals in the future, as evidenced by the development of edge AI and quantum-enhanced algorithms. The next generation of AI systems will be more capable, accountable, and approachable if human-centric design, ethical governance, and environmental sustainability are given top priority.

CHAPTER 3

BIOTECHNOLOGY DEVELOPMENTS

Over the past few decades, biotechnology has seen a significant transformation, moving from antiquated methods based on fermentation and agriculture to extremely complex contemporary inventions that make use of genetic research, molecular biology, and computational analysis. The transformative journey of biotechnology is examined in this chapter, including its historical development, significant advances in genetic research, the impact of genetic engineering and CRISPR technologies, the rise of synthetic biology and bioinformatics, and the profound innovations that are changing agriculture and medicine.

3.1 The Modern Era of Biotechnology

The current era of biotechnology is marked by a fast rate of invention and the merging of fields that were previously thought to be completely distinct. Understanding the evolution of biotechnology from its traditional roots to a discipline characterized by accuracy and technological integration is crucial to appreciating the contemporary landscape.

The Transition from Conventional Methods to Contemporary Innovation:

The origins of biotechnology can be traced back thousands of years to techniques like fermentation, selective breeding, and the use of therapeutic herbs. The foundation for comprehending and influencing biological processes for human advantage was established by these early methods. However, the development of molecular biology in the middle of the 20th century marked the beginning of the contemporary era of biotechnology.

Important turning points include:

The discovery of the structure of DNA:

- A vital basis for genetic study was established in 1953 when Watson and Crick clarified the double helix structure of DNA. This discovery paved the way for our current understanding of the storage, replication, and expression of genetic information.

Technology of Recombinant DNA:

- Scientists were able to cut, splice, and recombine genetic material from many organisms in the 1970s thanks to the invention of recombinant DNA technology. This resulted in the development of genetically modified organisms (GMOs), the bacterial production of human insulin, and a host of additional uses that revolutionized agriculture and medicine.

The Human Genome Project and High-Throughput Sequencing:

- Our knowledge of genetic information was completely transformed when the Human Genome Project was finished in the early 2000s. Advanced genetic diagnostics and tailored therapy were made possible by high-throughput sequencing technology, which significantly decreased the time and expense involved in decoding genetic data.

The following significant breakthroughs in genetic research and molecular biology have laid the groundwork for modern biotechnology:

- The 1980s saw the invention of PCR (Polymerase Chain Reaction), which allows for the quick amplification of particular DNA sequences. This method is essential to forensic science, diagnostics, and research.

- The creation of monoclonal antibodies has revolutionized the treatment of a variety of illnesses, including autoimmune disorders and cancer. These antibodies have great specificity and therapeutic efficacy because they are designed to target particular antigens.

- The development of next-generation sequencing has made it possible to analyze complete genomes quickly, which has improved our knowledge of evolutionary biology and allowed for the discovery of genetic variations linked to diseases.

- The development of enzymes and therapeutic proteins with improved stability and efficacy is the result of advancements in protein engineering, which include the use of computational techniques to design proteins with particular functionalities.

These developments highlight how contemporary biotechnology has evolved from a largely empirical field to one that is firmly anchored in technological innovation and scientific accuracy.

3.2 CRISPR and Genetic Engineering Technologies

One of the most innovative developments in contemporary biotechnology is genetic engineering. Among the instruments that have revolutionized this sector, CRISPR is one that is very powerful.

Gene Editing Principles and CRISPR's Function:

Genetic engineering is the intentional use of biotechnology to alter an organism's genome. Enhancing positive qualities, suppressing negative ones, or introducing whole new functions are all possible outcomes of the process.

This is the CRISPR-Cas9 system:

Originating from a bacterial immunity mechanism, the CRISPR-Cas9 system has transformed gene editing by providing previously unheard-of levels of accuracy, effectiveness, and user-friendliness. There are two primary parts to the system:

- A guide RNA (gRNA) is a brief RNA sequence that is intended to correspond with a certain DNA sequence found in the genome.
- The Cas9 enzyme is a nuclease that creates a double-strand break at the precise site that the gRNA specifies.

Action Mechanism:

The cell's natural healing mechanisms take over when the DNA is sliced, and they can be used to induce particular genetic alterations. These consist of:

- Gene disruption is frequently the outcome of insertions or deletions caused by non-homologous end joining (NHEJ).
- When a repair template is supplied, homology-directed repair (HDR) allows for the accurate insertion or correction of sequences.

Present Uses and Upcoming Opportunities:

The effects of CRISPR are being felt in several fields:

The field of medicinal therapeutics

- Genetic diseases include sickle cell anemia, muscular dystrophy, and some types of cancer are being treated via gene editing therapy. Promising outcomes from early clinical trials have opened the door for further uses.

The field of agricultural biotechnology

- Crops with improved nutritional profiles, increased production, and disease and insect resistance are being developed using CRISPR. As an illustration, crops can be modified to withstand drought, which is a crucial characteristic given climate change.
- Malnutrition in underdeveloped nations can be mitigated by fortifying staple foods with nutrients.

The Industrial Uses of:

CRISPR may find use in biofuels, waste management, and possibly environmental preservation in addition to health and agriculture. Scientists hope to increase the effectiveness of procedures like bioremediation by altering microbial ecosystems.

With CRISPR in particular, genetic engineering has a

bright future. Base editors and prime editing are two examples of next-generation gene editing technologies that researchers are eagerly investigating because they promise to increase precision and lessen off-target consequences. The limits of genetic manipulation will keep growing as these instruments advance, providing game-changing answers to some of the most difficult issues facing industry, agriculture, and health.

3.3 Bioinformatics and Synthetic Biology

In the interdisciplinary field of synthetic biology, new biological components, tools, and systems are designed and built by fusing concepts from computer science, engineering, and biology. In bioinformatics, however, biological data is analyzed and interpreted using computational techniques. When combined, these disciplines are expanding our understanding of and capacity for creating in the living world.

Generation of Synthetic Life Forms and Biomimetic Systems:

- The goal of synthetic biology is to either create

organisms that are not found in nature or rewire natural ones to carry out new tasks.

Construction and Design:

Standardized genetic components, commonly referred to as BioBricks, are used by researchers to construct biological circuits that have the ability to regulate cellular processes. New biological systems can be systematically assembled thanks to this modular methodology.

Scientists can create artificial systems that replicate biological processes by researching natural systems. Among the examples are:

- Artificial photosynthesis is a method of producing renewable energy by mimicking the natural process.
- Synthetic tissues are engineered tissues that can be used as drug test platforms or to replace injured organs.

Data Analytics and Computational Biology Driving Discovery:

- Bioinformatics is essential to synthetic biology because it analyzes large experimental datasets and makes it possible to rationally design novel systems.

- Massive volumes of data are produced by methods like next-generation sequencing, which is known as "high-throughput data analysis." This data is parsed with the use of bioinformatics tools, which uncover patterns that guide the creation of artificial biological circuits.

- **Modeling and Simulation:** By forecasting possible outcomes, computational models can model the behavior of artificial systems prior to their construction, saving time and resources.

Multi-Omics Data Integration:

Designing intricate synthetic systems requires a comprehensive understanding of biological processes, which bioinformatics provides by combining data from transcriptomics, proteomics, metabolomics, and genomes.

A new era of innovation is being fueled by synthetic biology and bioinformatics, which together are making it possible to create biological systems and organisms with unique designs. These fields improve our comprehension of the fundamental ideas of life itself in addition to making it possible to create new systems.

3.4 Biotechnological Advancements in Agriculture and Medicine

Perhaps the most obvious examples of the practical uses of contemporary biotechnology are found in the domains of agriculture and medicine, where advancements are not only revolutionizing existing procedures but also opening the door for new ones.

Transformative Impact on Personalized Medicine:
By enabling individual-tailored treatments, contemporary innovation has completely transformed the medical industry.

- **Genomic Medicine:** genomic predispositions to diseases can be identified thanks to advances in genomic sequencing. Using this data, individualized treatment programs that are catered to each patient's particular genetic composition are created.
- **Targeted Therapies:** Biotechnological advancements like CAR-T cell therapies and

monoclonal antibodies have produced medications that target particular disease pathways, greatly enhancing the prognosis for ailments including autoimmune disorders and cancer.

- **Regenerative medicine:** Advances in tissue engineering and stem cell research are opening the door to regenerative medicines that can replace or repair damaged organs and tissues.

Bullet Points on Benefits:

- Increased precision in diagnosis.
- Personalized treatment plans.
- Improved tracking of the effectiveness of treatment.
- Targeted therapies resulted in fewer side effects.

Agricultural Biotechnology Developments for Higher Yields and Sustainability:

- Biotechnology is spurring innovation in agriculture to address the problems posed by a changing climate and an expanding world population.
- **Crop Improvement:** Crop varieties that are more resistant to environmental stressors including drought, pests, and diseases are created through

genetic engineering procedures. These developments lessen the need for chemical pesticides and contribute to food security.

- **Nutritional Enhancement:** Biotechnology makes it possible to fortify crops with vital minerals and vitamins. To combat hunger in developing nations, Golden Rice, for instance, has been modified to include beta-carotene, a precursor of vitamin A.

- **Sustainable Farming Practices:** Biotechnology developments also support sustainable farming. Agricultural methods can be modified to minimize waste and environmental effect by utilizing biofertilizers and precision farming techniques.

The following are bullet points regarding agricultural innovations:

- Increased disease and pest resistance.
- The nutritional characteristics of main crops have improved.
- An increased capacity to withstand severe weather conditions.
- Via sustainable procedures, the environmental impact is lessened.

Medicine and agriculture are changing as a result of the combination of genetic engineering, biotechnology, and sophisticated computer techniques. Agricultural biotechnology is making sure that food supply is resilient and sustainable in the face of global difficulties, while personalized medicine is becoming a reality as treatments grow more tailored and focused.

In conclusion, the biotechnology developments discussed in this chapter point to a revolutionary period where contemporary innovation is reimagining long-standing patterns. From the development of molecular biology and genetic research to the introduction of revolutionary technologies like synthetic biology, CRISPR, and bioinformatics, contemporary biotechnology is opening up previously unimaginable possibilities. Furthermore, the observable advantages of better farming techniques and tailored medicine highlight the practical implications of these advancements.

As this subject continues to grow at a rapid pace, biotechnology has promise not only for solving present issues but also for radically changing how we think about food, health, and the environment. A future where the lines between biological and technological systems become less distinct and the world becomes more efficient, sustainable, and adaptable is being ushered in by researchers and practitioners who are utilizing the power of genetic engineering, synthetic biology, and advanced data analytics.

CHAPTER 4

SENSING TECHNOLOGIES AT THE CUTTING EDGE

Sensor technologies are the essential link between digital systems and the physical world in today's networked digital ecosystem. They supply the real-time data needed for automation, intelligent system reactions, and decision-making. This chapter explores the many functions of sensors in contemporary technology, including their development, integration with the Internet of Things (IoT), and specific uses in industrial operations, environmental monitoring, and biosensing.

4.1 Sensors' Function in a Digital Environment

Sensors are instruments that monitor and identify environmental changes, then translate these physical characteristics into signals that electronic systems can understand. Since they serve as the foundation for data collecting for a vast range of applications, their crucial role in contemporary digital ecosystems cannot be understated.

1. Description and Purpose:

Electronic parts called sensors are made to monitor and translate physical attributes like temperature, pressure, light, motion, or chemical makeup into electrical signals. After then, this signal can be broadcast, stored, or processed for additional examination. The significance of sensors is found in their capacity to:

- Record data from the real world in real time
- Supply the inputs required by automated systems
- Facilitate the shift from analog to digital analytics of phenomena.

2. A Synopsis of Sensor Types and Their Development:

From simple mechanical devices to extremely complex semiconductor-based systems, sensors have seen significant development. Important categories consist of:

- Thermostats and pressure gauges are examples of early mechanical sensors that functioned by physical movements.
- Electronic Sensors: By using integrated circuits and semiconductors, more accurate readings were made

possible. Accelerometers and photodiodes are two examples.

- Optical Sensors: Light-based change detection devices, such LIDAR and infrared sensors, which offer sophisticated imaging and mapping capabilities.
- Chemical Sensors: These sensors are crucial for applications such as medical diagnostics and air quality monitoring because they can identify changes in chemical composition.
- Biological Sensors (Biosensors): These sensors are essential for environmental monitoring and medical treatment since they are made to interact with biological factors.

The following traits have defined the evolution of sensors:

- **Miniaturization:** As sensors have gotten smaller, they can now be integrated into wearable and portable electronics.
- **Enhanced Sensitivity:** Sensors are now more accurate and precise thanks to better materials and design methods.

- **Wireless Connectivity:** In order to facilitate a smooth integration into Internet of Things networks, contemporary sensors frequently integrate wireless communication protocols.

- **Energy Efficiency:** Sensors that can run for long periods of time on little energy have been made possible by developments in low-power electronics.

4.2 Sensor networks and the Internet of Things

A revolutionary advancement that has completely changed how data is gathered, examined, and used in a variety of businesses is the incorporation of sensors into the Internet of Things (IoT).

1. Integration of Sensors into IoT Platforms:

The Internet of Things is a network of linked devices that exchange information online. In this ecosystem, sensors are the main elements that collect data. They are found in a wide variety of gadgets, including industrial machines, environmental monitoring stations, cellphones, and smartwatches. Important elements consist of:

- **Connectivity:** Sensors can connect to cellular

networks, Wi-Fi, Bluetooth, Zigbee, and other protocols.

- Data transmission in real time and with reliability is guaranteed by these communication protocols.
- **Data Aggregation:** A network of sensors can be formed to gather a variety of datasets.
- Centralized processing and analysis are made possible by the aggregation of data at edge devices or cloud platforms.
- **Automation and Control:** IoT systems can automatically modify settings in response to changes in the environment thanks to real-time sensor data. For instance, occupancy and outside temperature data are used by smart thermostats to modify heating and cooling.

The Transformative Impact of Real-Time Data Collection on Industries:

The capacity to gather data in real-time has important ramifications for various industries:

- **Smart Homes and Buildings:** Sensors keep an eye on temperature, lighting, and security systems, allowing for automatic control that improves comfort and energy efficiency.

- **Industrial Automation:** Sensor networks let manufacturers undertake predictive maintenance by tracking the performance of their equipment and anticipating faults before they happen.

- Production lines run more smoothly thanks to real-time monitoring, which also minimizes waste and downtime.

- **Transportation and Logistics:** IoT sensors monitor driver behavior, track vehicle locations, and optimize routes to cut fuel usage and enhance logistics.

- **Healthcare:** Wearable sensors gather health information, including heart rate and activity levels, which can be utilized for ongoing chronic condition monitoring and early diagnosis.

Precision agriculture, which optimizes productivity and reduces resource consumption, is made possible by sensor networks that track soil moisture, nutrient levels, and meteorological conditions.

Bullet Points Outlining Advantages:

- Increased effectiveness in operations.
- Enhanced security and decreased downtime.

- Making decisions in real time.
- Increased customization of goods and services.

4.3 Bioelectronic Interfaces and Biosensors

A specific class of sensors intended for direct interaction with biological systems are biosensors and bioelectronic interfaces. They play a key role in bridging the gap between environmental biology and digital technologies and human health.

1. Biosensor Design and Function:

In order to detect chemical or biological molecules, biosensors use biological elements like enzymes, antibodies, or cells. Usually, they are composed of three primary parts:

- The component that interacts with the target analyte (such as glucose oxidase in a blood sugar sensor) is known as a bioreceptor.
- The biorecognition event is transformed into an electrical signal via the transducer.
- Signal Processor: Processes and amplifies the signal, frequently transmitting the information to a remote

monitoring system or display.

2. Wearable and Implantable Devices:

Biosensors have been widely used in healthcare through those devices.

- **Wearable Biosensors:** Smartwatches and fitness trackers, among other devices, continuously monitor vital signs including blood oxygen levels, heart rate, and even stress markers.

- They support preventive healthcare initiatives and give users access to real-time health insights.

- **Implantable Biosensors:** Used for more important monitoring, like intracranial pressure in patients with neurological disorders or glucose levels in diabetic individuals.

- In an emergency, these gadgets can notify medical professionals and provide ongoing monitoring.

3. Keeping an eye on environmental and health parameters:

Personal health is just one aspect of bioelectronic interfaces. They are crucial to the monitoring of the environment:

- The use of biosensors in point-of-care diagnostics allows for the quick identification of infections or disease-related biomarkers.

- They facilitate prompt and precise diagnosis, which advances individualized medicine.

- Environmental Monitoring: Biosensors identify contaminants in water and air, such as pollution, poisons, or microbes.

- By offering vital information to guide repair tactics, they aid in environmental conservation initiatives.

4.4 Developments in Industrial and Environmental Sensing

Industrial operations and environmental monitoring have been significantly impacted by recent developments in sensor technology. Significant gains in operational efficiency and sustainability are being fueled by innovative sensor applications.

1. Environmental Monitoring Using Cutting-Edge Sensors:

Environmental sensors are vital weapons in the battle

against pollution and climate change. They offer vital information that influences industrial processes and policy.

- **Air Quality Monitoring:** Sensors quantify greenhouse gas emissions, volatile organic compounds (VOCs), and particulate matter (PM2.5 and PM10).

- Using real-time data facilitates the creation of pollution mitigation plans and the issuance of public health alerts.

- Monitoring of Water Quality and Soil: Advanced sensors examine nutrient content, pH levels, and chemical makeup.

- Monitoring agricultural fields and identifying water body contamination are two uses for this data.

- Conservationists can keep an eye on biodiversity and ecological health by using sensors to measure environmental elements in remote environments.

2. Innovations in Smart production and Industrial Sensing: Sensor technologies are revolutionizing the management and optimization of production processes in industrial settings.

- **Predictive Maintenance:** Sensors mounted on

equipment identify operating strains, temperature irregularities, and vibrations.

- By using this predictive method, businesses may reduce downtime and save money by doing maintenance before catastrophic failures occur.

- **Process optimization and quality control:** Sensors keep an eye on manufacturing factors in real time, guaranteeing that goods fulfill quality requirements.

- These sensors' data is utilized to optimize processes, increasing yield and decreasing waste.

3. Trends in Miniaturization, Energy Efficiency, and Wireless Communication:

Constant innovation in a number of crucial areas characterizes modern sensor technology:

- The development of ultra-small sensors that can be incorporated into a broad range of devices, from consumer electronics to industrial machinery, is the result of advancements in microelectromechanical systems (MEMS).

- **Energy Efficiency:** Sensors now use less power thanks to new materials and circuit designs, which extends battery life and even allows for energy harvesting.

- **Wireless Communication:** Sensors can send data over great distances with less power consumption thanks to the use of wireless technologies like Bluetooth Low Energy (BLE), Zigbee, and LoRaWAN. Building extensive sensor networks requires this connectivity, particularly in isolated or challenging-to-reach locations.

4. The Effect on Industry and Sustainability:

Sustainability is greatly enhanced by the use of cutting-edge sensors in industrial and environmental contexts:

- The efficient use of resources, including raw materials, electricity, and water, is made possible by real-time monitoring.

  Through dynamic process adjustments, enterprises can limit their environmental effect and eliminate waste.

  Enhanced Safety and Compliance: Ongoing data collection guarantees that industrial processes follow environmental and safety guidelines.

  Automated systems can react swiftly to dangerous

situations, safeguarding both the environment and human workers.

Advanced sensing technologies are transforming how we see and engage with the world. Sensors supply the vital information that drives innovation and decision-making, from their fundamental function in contemporary digital ecosystems to their complex uses in the Internet of Things, biosensing, environmental monitoring, and industrial automation. From the first mechanical devices to the sophisticated, compact, energy-efficient systems of today, sensor technology has seen a remarkable technical evolution.

These developments allow for major progress toward sustainability in addition to increased operational effectiveness and safety. Businesses and governments may make better decisions that encourage resource conservation and environmental stewardship by using sensors that continuously gather and send real-time data. Furthermore, while sophisticated industrial sensors provide quality control and predictive maintenance in production, biosensor integration into wearable and implantable devices is revolutionizing healthcare by enabling continuous monitoring and customized treatment.

Trends in wireless communication, energy efficiency, and shrinking will expand the possibilities and applications of sensor technology as it develops further. This chapter has examined the diverse functions of sensors and emphasized how crucial they are to advancing digital transformation in a number of industries. Advanced sensor technologies open the door to a smarter, more connected, and greener future in addition to bridging the gap between the digital and physical worlds.

CHAPTER 5

CONVERGENCE: COMBINING BIOTECHNOLOGY, AI, AND SENSOR INTEGRATION

A paradigm shift in the design, implementation, and management of complex systems is represented by the convergence of biotechnology, sensor technology, and artificial intelligence. This chapter investigates the theoretical foundations of this kind of integration, looks at real-world examples of successful convergence, explores the difficulties and approaches of data fusion for multimodal intelligence, and provides solutions for the problems that arise during smooth integration. These fields' convergence is more than just a mixing of technology; rather, it is a comprehensive strategy that builds on each discipline's advantages to produce intelligent, responsive, and adaptable systems.

5.1 Convergence Theoretical Framework

We must first look at the conceptual models that describe how these disparate domains come together to form a cohesive framework in order to comprehend the integration of AI, biotechnology, and sensors. This convergence is supported by a number of ideas and models.

1. Interdisciplinary Integration:

Conceptual Models of Convergence:

According to the convergence paradigm, there might be synergies that produce better results when different fields each with its own techniques, data formats, and applications intersect. For instance, biotechnology provides insights into the basic workings of life, sensors record data in real time, and artificial intelligence (AI) is excellent at processing massive datasets and forecasting outcomes. These domains can work together to create systems that are more responsive and dynamic than any one of them could be on its own.

Design of a Holistic System:

Convergence also highlights the necessity of holistic design, in which every part of a system is created with consideration for how it will interact with other parts. By encouraging cross-disciplinary collaboration rather than walled development, this strategy makes it possible to create inventions that are more powerful than the sum of their individual components.

Systems Theory:

- **Foundational Approaches:** Systems theory offers a framework for comprehending intricate interdependencies within integrated systems. It makes the argument that a system should not be seen as a collection of separate pieces but rather as an interconnected totality. Regarding convergence:

- A key feature of intelligent systems is constant learning and adaptation, which are made possible via feedback loops, which are highlighted by systems theory.

- New traits and capabilities that are not present in the individual components are created through integration. The idea of Living Intelligence, in which convergent technologies produce new functionality, is based on this emergent principle.

CPS stands for Cyber-Physical Systems.

Systems known as CPS closely combine physical operations with computational components. They are distinguished by:

- **Real-Time Interaction**: The capacity to perceive and react instantly to changes in the environment.
- The smooth exchange of information between sensors, computer systems, and actual actuators is known as interconnectivity.
- A key component in combining AI, biotechnology, and sensors into a single system is adaptive control, which is the ability to modify processes in response to changing data inputs.

These fundamental methods lay the theoretical groundwork for convergence by showing how several technologies can work together to improve performance, robustness, and creativity in a well-organized system.

5.2 Integrated Systems Case Studies

Applications of integrated systems in the real world offer

concrete proof of convergence's advantages. Case examples from a variety of industries, including healthcare, smart cities, and industrial automation, demonstrate how integrating biotechnology, AI, and sensor data may help resolve challenging issues.

1. Personalized Medicine:

Healthcare Integration:

To provide individualized treatment regimens, integrated systems in contemporary healthcare merge genetic data, biometric sensor readings, and AI-driven analytics. For example, wearable biosensors that continuously track vital signs and gather information on environmental conditions may be used by a patient with a chronic illness. Artificial intelligence (AI) systems process this data, compare it to a patient's genomic profile, and then suggest customized therapies or drug changes.

Remote Monitoring of Patients:

Patients with illnesses like diabetes or heart disease can now be monitored in real time thanks to telemedicine platforms that combine AI diagnoses with sensor data from home-based equipment. By facilitating the early identification of possible problems, this convergence not only enhances treatment outcomes but also lowers hospital readmission rates.

The following are bullet points about healthcare successes:

- Improved diagnostic precision via ongoing data tracking.
- Predictive analytics is used in early intervention and preventive treatment.
- Personalized treatment plans derived from thorough patient profiles.

2. Smart Cities and Urban Infrastructure:

Urban Planning and Environmental Monitoring:
Sensor networks are used in smart cities to track energy use, traffic, and air quality. City planners can maximize resource allocation, lower pollution, and enhance public services by combining this sensor data with AI analytics and, occasionally, biological indicators (like bioassays for water quality).

Management of Infrastructure:

Predictive maintenance of vital infrastructure, including roads and bridges, is made possible via integrated sensor networks. For instance, wear and stress data collected by sensors installed in roads and bridges is evaluated by AI systems to forecast maintenance requirements, averting breakdowns and increasing the lifespan of public infrastructure.

The following are bullet points about innovations in smart cities:

- Congestion has decreased and traffic management has improved.
- Waste management and energy use were optimized.
- The implementation of real-time monitoring has improved public safety.

3. Manufacturing and Industrial Automation:

Predictive Maintenance in Factories:

In industrial contexts, integrated systems anticipate equipment breakdowns before they happen by combining

AI algorithms with sensor data from machinery. This proactive strategy guarantees ongoing output, lowers maintenance expenses, and minimizes downtime.

Control of Quality:

Sensor integration with AI-powered visual inspection systems guarantees that goods fulfill exacting quality requirements. In semiconductor manufacturing, for example, sensors identify minute flaws while AI systems evaluate the information instantly, greatly lowering mistake rates.

Industrial Applications Bullet Points:

- Enhanced operational effectiveness and decreased operational expenses.
- Improved product quality via ongoing observation.
- Adaptive manufacturing processes are the result of real-time modifications.

5.3 Multimodal Intelligence and Data Fusion

Data fusion, or the process of combining many data kinds from various sources to create a cohesive, actionable understanding, is at the core of convergent systems. The methods and difficulties involved in data fusion and the creation of multimodal intelligence are examined in this section.

1. Methods for Combining Diverse Data Types:

- **Sensor Data Integration:** Data fusion techniques integrate data from several sensor types, including optical, pressure, and temperature sensors, to give a thorough picture of an environment. This is crucial for applications like smart agriculture, which require the synthesis of data from drones, weather stations, and soil sensors.

- **Multimodal Education:** AI systems are trained using data from multiple sources, including text, images, audio, and biological signals, in a process known as multimodal learning. As a result, the algorithm is able to comprehend context more thoroughly and generate predictions that are more accurate. For instance: To provide a comprehensive diagnosis, an AI system may examine genetic information in addition to medical imaging.

- The process of combining features taken from many

data sources into a single feature vector is known as "feature-level fusion."

- The process of combining the results of many models, each trained on a distinct modality, to reach a final judgment is known as "Decision-Level Fusion."

- **Hybrid Fusion Techniques:** To increase accuracy and resilience, a combination of feature and decision-level fusion is used.

2. Difficulties in Harmonizing Digital Signals with Biological Data:

- **Heterogeneity:** Digital sensor data and biological data are fundamentally different in terms of format, scale, and noise levels. Complex normalization and transformation methods are needed to integrate these various data kinds.

- **Alignment of Time:** It might be difficult to synchronize data streams that run on various time scales. For instance, sensor data can be continuous and real-time, while genetic data may be static.

- **Quality and Variability of Data:** Because of human variances, environmental influences, and measurement errors, biological data is frequently vulnerable to variability. For fusion to be effective, high-quality, consistent data must be guaranteed.

Bullet Points on Fusion Challenges:

- **Handling various sizes and data formats.**
- Time data from both static and dynamic sources can be synchronized.
- Handling the noise and variability that come with biological measurements.

5.4 Overcoming Obstacles in Integration

There are challenges in integrating biotechnology, sensing technologies, and artificial intelligence. Problems with latency, data security, and interoperability might prevent converged systems from operating well. However, these difficulties can be lessened by combining best practices with technological techniques.

1. Different Standards and Protocols:

Interoperability Issues:

- The absence of established protocols among various devices and systems is one of the main obstacles. Integration is challenging because biotech databases, sensor networks, and AI models frequently use disparate platforms and communication protocols.
- Adoption of universal standards and APIs is one of the strategies and solutions.
- The creation of middleware programs that serve as interpreters between several systems.
- Promoting industry cooperation in the creation of interoperable platforms.

2. Data Security and Privacy:

- **Sensitive Data Handling:** Converged systems frequently handle extremely sensitive data, particularly when combining real-time sensor data from personal devices with biological information.
- The use of strong encryption techniques for data storage and transmission is one of the security strategies.
- Frequent security audits and compliance checks for medical data with regulatory standards like HIPAA.

- In order to decrease single points of failure and lower the danger of significant data breaches, decentralized data processing systems are being developed.
- End-to-end encryption of data streams is one of the key points regarding data security.
- Safe authentication procedures for system and device access.
- Frequent security measures change in reaction to new threats.

3. Real-Time Integration Challenges:

Latency and Real-Time Processing:

- Real-time integration of data from several sources necessitates fast processing and low latency. Particularly in crucial applications like industrial automation and healthcare, delays in data processing can result in less-than-ideal choices.

The following are some strategies to lower latency:

- Using edge computing to process data nearer to the source.
- The utilization of high-speed communication

technologies and network infrastructure optimization.

- Making use of cloud-based tools for real-time, scalable data analysis.

Bullet Points on Latency Reduction:

- The use of edge devices for localized processing is one of the Bullet Points on Latency Reduction.
- Protocols for fast data transmission.
- Platforms for real-time analytics with reduced latency.

4. Future-Proofing Integrated Systems:

Scalability and Smooth Integration:

Scalability becomes crucial as the complexity of converging systems increases. Without sacrificing performance, systems must be built to manage growing volumes of data and more integrated components.

Methods for Reaching Scalability:

- The architecture of the system is modular, allowing for gradual integration.

- Infrastructures based on the cloud that provide elastic scalability.

- Adaptive algorithms and ongoing monitoring that can modify system performance in reaction to rising demand.

The way we develop and apply intelligent systems is changing dramatically as a result of the convergence of biotechnology, sensor technologies, and artificial intelligence. A strong theoretical basis for comprehending this integration is provided by systems theory and cyber-physical systems. Advanced methods in data fusion and multimodal intelligence show the possibilities and difficulties of integrating many data kinds, while real-world case studies in healthcare, smart cities, and industrial automation demonstrate the useful advantages of combining these technologies.

It takes a complex strategy that combines technology innovation, industry collaboration, and adherence to best practices to overcome integration obstacles, whether they be interoperability issues, data security concerns, or latency issues. Achieving smooth, scalable integration requires tactics like implementing edge computing, embracing universal standards, and making sure data security procedures are strong.

The opportunities and challenges presented by the convergence of biotechnology, sensor technologies, and artificial intelligence have been examined in this chapter. Future developments in healthcare, urban planning, industrial processes, and other areas will be reshaped by the effective fusion of various domains, which will also spur technical innovation. To fully realize Living Intelligence's potential and create systems that are more responsive, flexible, and able to tackle some of the most difficult issues of our day, it is essential to be able to harmonize various data kinds and get beyond integration obstacles.

CHAPTER 6

Uses in Personalized Medicine and Healthcare

One of the industries most likely to profit from the convergence of cutting-edge technologies is healthcare. This chapter examines the ways in which genetic profiling, biosensors, and artificial intelligence are transforming customized medicine and patient care. To guarantee that everyone benefits from technology advancement, we also go over the ethical and legal frameworks that need to change in step with these developments.

6.1 AI-Powered Diagnosis and Therapy

The methods used for diagnosis and treatment planning are being drastically changed by artificial intelligence. AI-driven systems are providing insights that were previously unattainable through the use of large datasets and potent algorithms.

1. Diagnostic Process Transformation:

Complex data processing and analysis are areas in which AI systems shine. They are utilized in diagnostics to:

- **Medical Imaging Interpretation:** The accuracy of deep learning models' analysis of X-rays, MRIs, CT scans, and ultrasounds is comparable to and occasionally better than that of human radiologists. These models identify minute patterns and irregularities that could point to early-stage illnesses including cancer, neurological issues, or heart conditions.

- **Electronic Health Records (EHRs) Analysis:** AI can find patterns and risk factors that human reviewers might miss by analyzing enormous volumes of medical data. Early diagnosis and more individualized treatment regimens may result from this investigation.

- **Supporting Pathology:** Pathologists can make speedier diagnosis by using AI-driven image analysis tools to more rapidly and reliably evaluate biopsy slides and other microscopic pictures.

2. Improving the Planning of Treatment:

AI aids in the creation of individualized treatment plans following a diagnosis:

- **The use of predictive analytics:** By combining real-time patient parameters with historical data, AI algorithms are able to forecast the course of diseases. Clinicians can use these predictions to assist them choose the best intervention techniques.

- **Systems for Decision Support:** By combining information from multiple sources, including imaging, laboratory testing, genetic profiles, and patient histories, integrated platforms give physicians insights that can be put to use. These systems make recommendations for treatments based on previous clinical results and evidence-based guidelines.

- **Personalized Treatment Plans:** AI makes it possible to create treatment regimens that are precisely tailored to each patient's needs by taking into account their distinctive traits. This is especially important for complicated illnesses like cancer, where people' reactions to treatment can differ greatly.

Highlights of AI-Driven Advantages:

- Quicker and more precise diagnosis.

- A decrease in diagnostic mistakes.

- Simplified planning for therapy.

- Therapy is adjusted in real time according to patient response.

3. An example of a case:

Think about an oncology facility where AI is incorporated into the process of diagnosing patients. A deep learning algorithm automatically analyzes a patient's imaging results and identifies worrisome spots. At the same time, a decision-support system processes the patient's EHR data, including genetic markers and past treatment results. The integrated analysis helps the oncologist choose a tailored therapy plan that maximizes patient outcomes by confirming the existence of a malignant tumor and forecasting its aggressiveness.

6.2 Biosensors' Effect on Patient Monitoring

The collection and utilization of patient data in clinical

treatment is being completely transformed by biosensors. These gadgets, which range from wearables to implanted sensors, make it possible to continuously and instantly monitor a large number of physiological characteristics.

1. Transforming Ongoing Health Monitoring:

Biosensors enable better disease management and early intervention by giving a dynamic picture of a patient's health.

- The wearable sensors are: Heart rate, blood oxygen levels, physical activity, and sleep patterns are all monitored by sensors found in gadgets like fitness trackers and smartwatches. This continuous flow of information is very helpful in identifying health problems early on.

- **Implantable Devices:** Implantable biosensors give continuous data that may be sent to medical professionals. These sensors are used to monitor intracranial pressure in people with neurological disorders or glucose levels in diabetic patients. This is essential for preventing crises and managing long-term illnesses.

- **Remote Monitoring of Patients:** Biosensor data

can now be integrated into remote patient monitoring systems thanks to developments in telemedicine. Real-time tracking of vital signs and other health variables allows clinicians to make timely treatment adjustments based on up-to-date information.

2. Data Analytics in Real-Time:

Advanced analytics is used to process the data gathered by biosensors, increasing its usefulness:

- **Predictive alerts and trend analysis:** Before a crisis arises, trends that point to a decline in health can be found thanks to continuous data streams. An imminent cardiac event, for example, may be indicated by minute variations in heart rate variability.

- **AI Integration:** Predictive analytics that anticipate health events can be obtained by combining biosensor data with AI algorithms. Effective resource allocation and patient care prioritization are made possible by this combination.

- **Customized Comments:** Based on their real-time data, patients receive tailored insights and suggestions. They may be more inclined to follow treatment guidelines and adopt healthier lifestyle choices as a result of this feedback.

Bullet Points on the Impact of Biosensors:

- Vital metrics are continuously and in real time monitored.
- Prompt identification of possible health problems.
- Improved adherence and patient involvement.
- A decrease in emergency interventions and readmissions to hospitals.

3. An example of a case:

Wearable biosensors that continually monitor vital signs like blood pressure, heart rate, and fluid retention are given to heart failure patients as part of a chronic illness management program. A centralized platform receives this data, where AI systems examine patterns and identify irregularities. The technology notifies medical professionals when a possible risk is detected, allowing them to take early action perhaps by changing prescriptions or setting up a teleconsultation to avoid hospitalization and enhance patient quality of life.

6.3 Genetic Profiling for Personalized Medicine

A developing field called "personalized medicine" adjusts medical care to each patient's unique traits. A key component of this strategy is genetic profiling, which provides information about how a patient's genetic composition affects how they react to particular medicines.

1. Including Genetic Information in Treatment Plans:

Analyzing a person's DNA to find particular markers that may affect their risk of developing a disease and how well they respond to therapy is known as genetic profiling.

The process of genomic sequencing:

Rapid and economical decoding of a patient's genetic information is now feasible thanks to next-generation sequencing technologies. This information offers a framework for comprehending disease susceptibilities.

Identifying Biomarkers:

Certain biomarkers or genetic variations can forecast a patient's reaction to a certain treatment. For instance, the effectiveness of a targeted therapy may depend on specific mutations in cancer cells.

Personalized Treatment Plans:

Clinicians can create treatment plans that are tailored to each patient by using genetic data. For individuals at high genetic risk, this may entail choosing drugs that are most likely to work, modifying dosages, or even choosing to take preventative action.

The following are bullet points about personalized medicine:

- A thorough genomic analysis to determine each person's unique risk.
- Personalized therapy regimens according to genetic markers.
- Improved effectiveness and fewer side effects.
- Possibilities for preventative care and early intervention.

2. The Potential of Customized Treatments:

The goal of personalized medicine is to abandon the "one-size-fits-all" method and adopt tactics that take into account each patient's particular genetic profile.

Treating Cancer:

Genetic profiling is transforming cancer treatment in oncology. Oncologists can recommend treatments that target the precise pathways that cause tumor growth by knowing the genetic alterations that cause them. This reduces negative side effects while simultaneously improving results.

The field of pharmacogenomics:

This area of study looks at how a person's genes impact how they react to medications. By using pharmacogenomic data, doctors may anticipate which drugs and dosages would work best for a particular patient, eliminating the trial-and-error process that comes with writing prescriptions.

The field of preventive medicine:

Individuals at high risk for specific illnesses can be identified through genetic screening, enabling early intervention and customized preventive measures. For example, specific lifestyle changes and preventative drugs may be beneficial for patients with a high genetic risk of cardiovascular disease.

3. An example of a case:

Think about a patient who has been given a breast cancer diagnosis. Clinicians discover a mutation in the BRCA gene that dramatically raises the chance of recurrence through thorough genetic analysis. Equipped with this knowledge, the medical staff creates a customized treatment strategy that consists of hormone therapy, targeted chemotherapy, and ongoing genetic testing. In addition to improving the patient's prognosis, this customized strategy lowers needless exposure to potentially ineffective medicines.

6.4 Medical Ethical and Regulatory Considerations

The ethical and regulatory aspects of medical innovation are becoming more and more important as technology develops at a never-before-seen rate. Concerns around privacy, informed permission, data protection, and the moral use of technology must be addressed because of its uses in personalized medicine, diagnostics, and treatment planning.

1. Data Protection and Privacy Issues:

Highly sensitive personal data must be gathered and analyzed in order to integrate AI, biosensors, and genetic data in healthcare.

The confidentiality of patients:

It's critical to protect patient privacy. Strong data security protocols, such as encryption and safe data storage, are necessary to prevent unwanted access to patient data.

Conscientious Consent:

Patients need to know exactly what information is being gathered, how it will be used, and who will be able to access it. A basic ethical need that guarantees patients are aware of the advantages and disadvantages of new technologies is informed consent.

The following are bullet points regarding data protection and privacy:

- End-to-end encryption is used when transmitting data.

- The application of safe storage techniques.
- Clear guidelines for the use and exchange of data.
- Frequent audits and adherence to privacy laws.

2. Ethical guidelines and regulatory frameworks:

In order to guarantee the safe and moral application of technical developments, regulatory frameworks are essential.

The current rules are as follows:

Guidelines for data protection in healthcare are provided by legislation like the General Data Protection Regulation (GDPR) in Europe and the Health Insurance Portability and Accountability Act (HIPAA) in the United States in various locations. But as technology advances, these rules need to be revised to take into account new issues.

New Guidelines Are Needed:

New legal frameworks that strike a balance between innovation and individual rights protection are necessary given the speed at which biotechnology and artificial intelligence are developing.

The following are ethical considerations:

Ethical standards ought to cover:

- **Bias and Fairness:** Making sure algorithms don't produce biased results or reinforce pre-existing biases.
- **Transparency:** Creating interpretable and explicable mechanisms that help patients and clinicians comprehend the decision-making process.
- **Accountability:** Clearly defining who is responsible for what when clinical decision-making involves technology.

Regulatory Focus Bullet Points:

- Laws pertaining to data privacy are constantly being updated.
- Policymakers, technologists, and medical experts working together.
- The creation of moral frameworks that are adapted to new technologies.
- Making certain that patient rights are given top priority in all technological applications.

3. The Function of Oversight and Ethical Committees:

Many healthcare organizations have set up ethics committees and oversight bodies to help them negotiate the complicated ethical terrain. These teams are in charge of:

- Examining clinical procedures and innovative technologies.
- Making certain that clinical applications and research follow ethical guidelines.
- Giving advice on complicated situations when patient care and technological innovation collide.
- Interacting with patients and the general public to foster trust and guarantee that moral principles are in line with cultural norms.

4. An example of a case:

A hospital must go through a thorough evaluation procedure before deploying a new AI-driven diagnostic tool. This procedure entails:

- Assessing the AI system's fairness and accuracy.
- Ensuring the anonymization and safe storage of all patient data utilized for deployment and training.
- Trials are being carried out to compare results with conventional diagnostic techniques.

- Setting up procedures for open communication with patients and informed consent.

- Collaborating with regulatory organizations to guarantee adherence to current rules and regulations.

- This all-encompassing strategy guarantees that technical developments are applied morally and sensibly, protecting patient rights and improving clinical care.

In summary, the field of patient care and personalized medicine is changing as a result of the incorporation of AI, biosensors, and genetic profiling. Faster, more precise, and more individualized interventions are being made possible by AI-driven diagnoses and treatment planning, while biosensors offer ongoing monitoring that empowers both patients and medical professionals. Customized medicines that take into account each patient's distinct genetic composition are becoming possible thanks to genetic profiling, which guarantees that treatments are both efficient and minimally invasive. But these developments also bring with them important moral and legal issues that need to be resolved by strong data security protocols, open business practices, and modernized legal frameworks.

All parties involved clinicians, researchers, legislators, and patients must collaborate as healthcare continues to change in response to technology advancements in order to guarantee that the advantages of these developments are distributed properly. Although tailored treatment and improved diagnostics hold great potential, they must be weighed against a dedication to privacy, moral behavior, and ongoing regulatory standard development. This coordinated strategy will contribute to the development of a future in which technology maintains the greatest standards of patient care and ethical integrity while simultaneously advancing medical knowledge.

CHAPTER 7

Environmental Monitoring and Smart Cities

The future of urban living is represented by smart cities, which combine sustainable practices, infrastructure, and technology to produce more livable, efficient, and ecologically conscious urban settings. This chapter examines how sensors, artificial intelligence (AI), and data-driven decision-making might revolutionize environmental monitoring and urban planning. We look at how these technologies assist real-time environmental monitoring, how they aid in resource optimization and maintenance requirement prediction, and how they are incorporated into smart city infrastructure. Lastly, we discuss the important policy, privacy, and security issues raised by the extensive gathering and use of urban data.

7.1 Sensor Integration and Urban Planning

The incorporation of cutting-edge sensor technologies has

drastically changed modern urban planning. Today, sensors are essential for gathering information on almost every facet of urban life, from energy use to traffic flow, allowing planners to create and run cities in previously unthinkable ways.

1. Urban Infrastructure Transformation:

Real-time monitoring and analysis of the dynamic situations of urban settings is made possible by sensors integrated into urban infrastructure. This integration makes it easier to:

Smart Grids:

A network of sensors is used by smart grids to track energy use in various neighborhoods, dynamically modify energy distribution, and effectively integrate renewable energy sources. Utilities can manage load balancing, identify defects, and improve energy use thanks to the data gathered.

Systems for managing traffic:

In order to collect information on traffic volumes, speeds, and congestion patterns, modern cities install sensors on roads, at intersections, and within cars. This data is utilized to:

- Real-time traffic signal adjustments.
- Reduce traffic congestion and improve traffic flow.
- To prevent delays, give commuters dynamic routing recommendations.

Systems for Monitoring Energy:

Energy consumption is measured by sensors installed in infrastructure, streetlights, and public buildings, which aids in locating inefficiencies and potential improvement areas. This information is necessary for:

- Putting energy-saving strategies into action.
- Cutting carbon emissions in general.
- Improving urban operations' sustainability.

2. Urban planning's role:

Urban planning has become increasingly data-driven since the introduction of sensor integration. Now, planners can use real-time data to:

Constructing Resilient Infrastructure:

Cities may anticipate and stop infrastructure disasters by

using vibration and stress sensors to monitor the structural health of their buildings. Bridges, tunnels, and public buildings are examples of vital assets that are kept safe and functional using this proactive maintenance method.

Enhance Public Services:

The effective management of public transit, water distribution, and waste collection is made possible by sensor data, which guarantees that resources are distributed where they are most needed.

Increase Citizen Involvement:

Open data programs promote transparency and public involvement in urban development projects by giving individuals access to up-to-date information about their city.

- Highlights of the Advantages of Sensor Integration:
- Insights on urban dynamics in real time.
- Enhanced effectiveness in the distribution of resources.
- Improved security and less downtime for vital infrastructure.

- Planning based on data promotes sustainable urban expansion.

7.2 AI in Sustainability and Infrastructure Management

In smart cities, artificial intelligence is quickly taking center stage in infrastructure management. AI can forecast maintenance requirements, maximize resource utilization, and promote sustainable urban development by evaluating data from sensor networks.

1. The use of predictive maintenance

In order to predict possible breakdowns before they happen, artificial intelligence algorithms examine data from sensors integrated into municipal infrastructure. This proactive strategy lowers maintenance expenses and downtime. For instance:

The monitoring of bridges:

AI systems can anticipate when a bridge may need reinforcement or maintenance thanks to sensors that identify changes in stress and vibration patterns.

Maintenance of Roadways:

Road conditions, including surface deterioration and pothole formation, can be continuously monitored to enable prompt repairs, improving public safety and lowering long-term repair expenses.

2. Resource Utilization Optimization:

The effective management of urban resources is made possible by AI's capacity to interpret enormous volumes of sensor data in real time. Important uses consist of:

Management of Energy:

By examining usage trends throughout the smart grid, AI algorithms improve the allocation of energy. They can reduce energy waste by dynamically adjusting the power distribution according to supply and demand.

The distribution of water:

Water utilities can optimize distribution and reduce water loss by using AI algorithms to monitor usage and leaks through a network of sensors.

Streamlining Traffic:

Real-time data is used by AI-powered traffic management systems to modify traffic signals, ease congestion, and enhance vehicle flow in general. In addition to saving commuters' time, this lowers pollutants from idling automobiles.

3. Case Studies of Initiatives for Sustainable Cities:

To encourage sustainability, a number of cities worldwide have put AI-driven infrastructure management systems into place:

The Smart Nation Initiative in Singapore:

AI has been included into Singapore's urban planning to control waste collection, energy use, and transportation. The city-state monitors environmental conditions, anticipates maintenance needs, and optimizes public transit routes using a network of sensors and AI analytics.

Barcelona's Urban Mobility Initiative:

AI is being used in Barcelona to evaluate traffic data and improve public transit, which lowers carbon emissions and congestion. Better urban air quality and more efficient traffic flow are the outcomes of this program.

The following are bullet points on AI in sustainability:

- Predictive maintenance can lower operating expenses.
- Improved water and energy management.
- Enhanced traffic flow results in lower emissions.
- Decisions based on data that support sustainability over the long run.

7.3 Environmental Monitoring in Real Time

One of the most important uses of sensor networks in smart cities is real-time environmental monitoring, which provides the information required to reduce environmental risks and advance sustainability.

1. Sensor Network Implementation:

Urban areas are equipped with sophisticated sensor networks to continuously monitor environmental conditions. These networks gather information on:

The quality of the air:

Pollutants including sulfur dioxide, nitrogen dioxide, particulate matter (PM2.5, PM10), and volatile organic compounds (VOCs) are all measured using sensors. When evaluating air quality and sending out public health alerts, this information is crucial.

Quality of Water:

Parameters including pH, turbidity, dissolved oxygen, and pollutant levels are monitored by sensors placed in water bodies and treatment plants. Healthy aquatic ecosystems and clean drinking water depend on these measures.

The quality of the soil:

Soil sensors track pollution, moisture content, and nutrient levels in both urban and agricultural environments. This information supports sustainable farming methods and aids in land use management.

2. Making Decisions Based on Data to Reduce Environmental Risks:

Environmental agencies and civic leaders can make well-informed judgments thanks to the constant flow of environmental data:

Systems for Early Warning:

The development of early warning systems for environmental threats like increases in air pollution, water contamination incidents, or soil degradation is made possible by real-time data. These technologies notify the public and authorities, enabling timely corrective action.

The development of policy:

The creation of focused policies meant to lower pollution and encourage sustainable activities is supported by comprehensive environmental monitoring data. For instance, low-emission zones or congestion pricing may be implemented as a result of data on emissions related to traffic.

In terms of resource management:

Strategies for conserving resources, such the creation of green spaces in cities or precision irrigation in agriculture, can be informed by data on soil and water quality.

3. An example of a case:

Think about a coastal city that frequently struggles with

water quality and air pollution. To keep an eye on water pollutants in adjacent coastal areas, automobile exhaust, and industrial emissions, a network of environmental sensors has been placed across the city. An AI system analyzes the gathered data in real time, looking for trends and forecasting possible environmental hazards. The technology sends out notifications when pollutant levels are above permissible limits, which prompts local officials to take corrective action, like limiting industrial operations or warning citizens about their health. This proactive strategy promotes long-term environmental sustainability in addition to protecting public health.

7.4 Smart Cities: Policy, Privacy, and Security

Significant issues with cybersecurity, privacy, and governance arise from the massive data collecting in smart cities. Creating strong legal and policy frameworks that safeguard citizens and promote innovation is crucial.

1. Difficulties in Governance:
Every day, millions of data points are created, making it difficult to manage and administer this data:

Transparency and Data Ownership:

One of the biggest challenges is figuring out who owns the data that sensors acquire and how to use it. Establishing confidence between citizens and governing entities requires openness in data collection procedures.

The coordination of interagency efforts:

Many parties, including public and commercial organizations, are frequently involved in smart cities. Effective data management and equitable distribution of the advantages of smart city projects depend on concerted efforts.

Government Bullet Points:

- Unambiguous rules on data ownership.
- Clear and open reporting procedures.
- Multi-stakeholder oversight that is coordinated.

2. Privacy Issues:

There are serious privacy concerns with the gathering of comprehensive, real-time data about urban settings and citizen behavior:

Protecting Personal Information:

It is crucial to make sure that any personal information gathered by sensors, whether it pertains to a person's movements, health indicators, or internet activity is shielded from abuse.

Consent and Anonymization:

Strong consent procedures and efficient anonymization methods are necessary to guarantee that citizens' privacy is maintained. People must be able to choose whether or not to participate in data collection activities.

- The following are bullet points on privacy measures:
- The application of data anonymization techniques.
- Systems for managing consent.
- Frequent evaluations of the impact on privacy.

3. Protections Against Cybersecurity:

Smart cities are more susceptible to cyberattacks as a result of their increased connectivity. Strong cybersecurity defenses are necessary to safeguard data integrity and vital infrastructure functionality.

Strategies for Mitigating Risk:

In smart cities, cybersecurity entails safeguarding networks against unwanted access and making sure data is transferred safely. Some strategies are:

Encryption:

To avoid unwanted access, data should be encrypted both during storage and transmission.

Controls of Access:

putting in place stringent authentication procedures and access restrictions to restrict who has access to private information.

Consistent Security Audits:

Regular audits and ongoing monitoring assist in locating weaknesses and guaranteeing that security protocols are current.

Cybersecurity Bullet Points:
- Protocols for end-to-end encryption.
- Authentication with many factors.
- Systems for ongoing surveillance and threat identification.

4. Regulatory Structures:

To strike a balance between the advantages of smart city technologies and the requirement to uphold individuals' rights, effective regulation is crucial:

Recent Law Updates:

The new realities of digital data collecting and processing need updating current privacy and data protection regulations. A foundation is provided by laws like the GDPR in Europe and HIPAA in the US, but more work is required to handle the particular difficulties presented by smart cities.

Cooperation Amongst Stakeholders:

To develop robust and adaptable regulatory frameworks, governments, business executives, and civil society organizations must collaborate. Standards that guarantee data is utilized securely and ethically may result from this collaboration.

Regulatory Focus Bullet Points:

- Current data protection laws should be revised.

- Collaboration among stakeholders to establish standards.
- Ensuring regulatory adaptability to new developments in technology.

A key component of smart cities is the incorporation of sensor technology into environmental monitoring and urban planning, which is revolutionizing the way cities are planned, run, and maintained. Urban planners may create robust, effective, and sustainable infrastructure systems that maximize resource utilization and improve inhabitants' quality of life by integrating sensors, artificial intelligence, and data analytics. Critical information that can reduce environmental risks and guide policy decisions is provided by real-time monitoring of environmental factors like soil, water, and air quality.

When combined with sophisticated sensor networks, artificial intelligence's contribution to infrastructure management enabling predictive maintenance and optimizing resource allocation has resulted in the development of eco-friendly and productive smart cities. But there are also serious drawbacks to these technical developments, especially when it comes to cybersecurity, privacy, and legislation. To safeguard citizens and promote innovation, strong governance structures, modern regulatory measures, and strict privacy and security standards must be put in place.

The combination of these technologies in smart cities is not just a pipe dream; it is already a reality that is changing urban environments all over the world. The future of urban living is expected to be more intelligent, flexible, and responsive than ever before, with an emphasis on data-driven decision-making, sustainable resource management, and citizen-centric government. Although there are many obstacles to overcome, there are also many potential advantages with careful planning and cooperation, which bodes well for a time when cities are not just intelligent but also sustainable, safe, and welcoming.

CHAPTER 8

EDUCATION, EMPLOYMENT, AND SOCIAL CONSEQUENCES

In addition to changing industries and healthcare, the confluence of AI, biotechnology, sensor technology, and other cutting-edge technologies is also having a significant impact on education, the workforce, and society at large. This chapter examines how Living Intelligence is changing job development, changing educational methods, and posing both opportunities and problems for society. We also go into how important ethical governance and public policy are in directing these revolutionary developments.

8.1 Using Adaptive Learning Systems to Transform Education

A new era of individualized, adaptable learning is being ushered in by the integration of Living Intelligence, which is fundamental to the advancement of society. Conventional educational models have frequently depended on uniform teaching techniques and standardized curriculum that fail to take into consideration the unique needs of each student. AI-powered adaptive learning systems have made it possible to customize instruction to each student's particular interests, pace, and learning style.

1. Customizing Instructional Materials and Approaches:

Real-time data and sophisticated analytics are used by adaptive learning systems to modify course material based on student performance. This customization is accomplished by:

Insights Based on Data:

To determine strengths and shortcomings, AI algorithms examine student performance data, including quiz scores, assignment grades, and engagement levels. Each learner will receive lessons that are neither too difficult nor too easy thanks to the content personalization informed by this study.

Dynamic Delivery of Content:

Adaptive systems offer customized pathways in place of a

curriculum that is one-size-fits-all. For instance, the system can provide extra resources and focused workouts to help students who perform well in arithmetic but poorly in language arts.

Modules for Interactive Learning:

To improve learning, digital platforms incorporate multimedia content, gamification, and interactive simulations. These modules ensure maximum learning efficiency by varying in complexity according to the student's responses.

Highlights of the Advantages of Personalization:

- Learning experiences that are tailored to each student's needs.
- Improved student involvement with interactive materials.
- Curriculum changes made in real time in response to performance data.
- Better academic results as a result of customized learning pathways.

2. Real-time feedback mechanisms and AI tutoring

systems:

AI tutoring programs simulate the advantages of individualized learning by offering pupils one-on-one assistance. These systems provide a number of benefits.

The following is immediate feedback:

Students are given rapid feedback on their work, which enables them to recognize and fix errors right away. Learning and retention are accelerated by this ongoing feedback loop.

Scalable Assistance:

By serving thousands of students at once, AI tutors can close the gap in teacher-to-student ratios and guarantee that all students have access to high-quality instruction.

The use of adaptive remediation

The AI tutor can offer extra materials, practice problems, or different explanations when a learner is having trouble understanding a particular idea until mastery is attained.

Highlights of the Advantages of AI Tutoring:

- Personalized care free from the restrictions imposed

by human resource shortages.

- Improved comprehension via iterative feedback.
- Learning gaps are lessened, and academic confidence is raised.
- Scalability to accommodate extensive educational systems.

Incorporating adaptive learning technology not only transforms conventional classroom environments but also makes high-quality education accessible to underprivileged and rural areas. Education becomes more effective, efficient, and entertaining by utilizing data-driven insights and individualized feedback, thereby equipping students for a fast changing future.

8.2 Training Employees in a Converged Technology Environment

The nature of labor is radically changing as Living Intelligence emerges. The workforce must adapt to new demands as industries grow more technologically advanced. This evolution necessitates a change in skill sets, ongoing education, and proactive tactics to keep workers competitive in a labor market that is changing quickly.

1. Examining the Competencies Needed in Developing Employment Markets:

There is a need for new abilities that combine technical know-how with soft skills as a result of the incorporation of innovative technology into routine company operations. Among the essential skills are:

Proficiency in technical aspects:

Employees must have a firm grasp of data analytics, programming languages, and digital tools. Knowledge of AI and machine learning is becoming more and more important as these technologies proliferate.

Multidisciplinary Expertise:

Because different industries are coming together, workers need to learn how to work across disciplines. For instance, in order to properly use AI, healthcare personnel might need to be knowledgeable with both medical science and data analytics.

The ability to solve problems creatively:

Critical thinking and creative problem-solving skills are highly regarded. This ability is particularly crucial as mundane tasks are automated, freeing up human intelligence to tackle increasingly difficult problems.

Adaptability and Ongoing Education:

Because of the speed at which technology is developing, lifelong learning is now required rather than elective. Employees need to be able to refresh their skill sets on a regular basis and adjust to new technology.

Emerging Skills Bullet Points:

- Data analysis and digital literacy.
- The interdisciplinary integration of domain-specific knowledge and technology.
- The ability to solve problems and think creatively.
- Flexibility and a dedication to lifelong learning.

2. Initiatives for Lifelong Learning and Reskilling:

Initiatives for reskilling and upskilling become increasingly important for workforce development as technology advances. Governments and organizations need to fund initiatives that equip workers for the jobs of the future.

Programs for Corporate Training:

Nowadays, a lot of businesses provide internal training programs to assist staff in learning new skills. Digital tools, AI applications, and other cutting-edge technologies are frequently the focus of these programs.

Public-Private Collaborations:

Working together, government organizations, academic institutions, and private businesses can develop extensive reskilling initiatives that close the skills gap nationally.

Platforms for Online Learning:

Employees now find it simpler to pursue lifelong learning because of the growth of online education. Employees can study at their own speed with courses on a variety of subjects, from blockchain technology to data science, offered by platforms like Coursera, edX, and Udacity.

Lifelong Learning Bullet Points:

- Industry and government cooperation to finance training programs.

- Online courses that are accessible, adaptable, and enable lifelong learning.

- To get ready for multifunctional roles, concentrate on developing both soft and technical abilities.

- Programs for mentorship and support during career transitions.

Organizations can make sure that their workforce is competitive, adaptable, and prepared to handle the demands of a convergent digital world by cultivating a culture of proactive skill development and ongoing learning. In addition to helping individual workers, this emphasis promotes innovation and more general economic growth.

8.3 The Effects of Living Intelligence on Society

The societal ramifications of Living Intelligence's broad acceptance are profound. These technologies have the ability to boost productivity and enhance quality of life, but they also come with drawbacks that need to be controlled to avoid injustices and disturbances.

1. Positive Shifts in Society:

The way people live, work, and interact with their surroundings can be greatly enhanced by the combination of biotechnology, sensor technology, and artificial intelligence.

A higher standard of living:

- Improved medical care by ongoing monitoring and tailored treatment.
- Smart cities have more effective infrastructure and public services.
- Adaptive learning methods make education more accessible.

Innovation and Economic Growth:

- Productivity gains and the opening of new positions in developing industries.
- The development of creative startups that tackle difficult societal issues.
- Environmental Advantages:
- Monitoring the environment in real time can help reduce pollution and improve resource management.
- AI and data analytics-driven sustainable practices

can help create a more environmentally friendly economy.

2. Potentially Harmful Shifts in Society:

Despite the advantages, there may be unforeseen repercussions when cutting-edge technologies come together:

The Digital Divide and Inequities:

Existing socioeconomic inequities may be made worse by the speed at which technology is developing. People who have access to cutting-edge technologies can gain disproportionately, leaving behind groups with less resources or digital knowledge.

The Automation and Displacement of Jobs:

AI and robotics-driven automation has the potential to eliminate jobs, especially in industries where repetitive operations can be readily automated. Strong reskilling and job transfer initiatives are therefore required.

Social Disturbances:

Rapid advancements in technology have the potential to

cause social unrest by altering community structures, family relationships, and general social standards. There's a chance that technology will advance faster than social structures can adjust.

Alert Points on Adverse Effects:
- The digital divide between various socioeconomic categories is growing.
- Possible automation-related employment losses.
- As conventional roles and systems change, there are social and cultural upheavals.
- The difficulties in guaranteeing fair access to the advantages of technology.

The effects of living intelligence on society are intricate and varied. Although there is enormous promise for improved sustainability, creativity, and well-being, there is also an urgent need to address the issues that could result in greater inequality and social unrest. It is imperative to implement proactive strategies in public policy, workforce development, and education to guarantee that the advantages of emerging technologies are shared equitably throughout society.

8.4 Ethical Governance and Public Policy

Public policy and ethical governance must keep up with the rapid changes brought about by Living Intelligence in the fields of education, the workforce, and society. To guarantee that technical breakthroughs are applied responsibly and fairly, strong frameworks are required.

1. Examination of Present Policies:

Numerous nations have put in place legislative frameworks to control various facets of technology use, including guidelines for AI ethics and data protection legislation like GDPR and HIPAA. But these regulations frequently fall behind the pace of technological development.

Pre-existing Structures:

- Rules pertaining to privacy and data protection.
- Guidelines for the moral application of AI in the financial, medical, and other domains.

The following are regulatory gaps:

- Rapid technological convergence produces situations

that are not entirely covered by current legislation.

- New regulations are required that take into account how biotechnology, AI, and sensor data are integrated.

2. Putting Forward Structures for Conscientious Innovation:

New legal frameworks that strike a balance between the protection of human rights and community values and technical growth are necessary to promote responsible innovation.

Creation of Inclusive Policies:

- Involve government, business, academic, and civil society players in the formulation of public policy.
- Form advisory groups including representatives from the community, technologists, and ethicists.

Ethical AI and Biotechnology Guidelines:

- Provide thorough criteria that cover sustainability, accountability, transparency, and equity.
- Encourage the development of standards that guarantee AI systems can be explained, biases are

reduced, and decision-making procedures are open.

Key Takeaways on Policy Initiatives:

- Cooperative policymaking with a variety of stakeholders.
- Regulations are continuously reviewed and updated.
- The creation of moral standards tailored to convergent technology.
- The execution of compliance audits and accountability procedures.

3. The function of academia, industry, and government:

All important stakeholders must work together to effectively regulate living intelligence:

Government:

- Establish rules that safeguard the public and encourage creativity.
- To keep ahead of new issues, spend money on research & development.
- Funding and incentives should be made available for the development of ethical technologies.

Industry:

- Adopt ethical AI, transparency, and data security best practices.

- Work together with legislators to create regulations that take into account real-world situations.

- To get ready for a convergent tech landscape, fund worker development programs.

Education:

- Investigate the societal effects of developing technology by doing transdisciplinary study.

- Teach ethical and responsible innovation to the upcoming generation of professionals.

- By offering guidance on policy and regulatory issues, you can act as a link between theoretical research and real-world application.

In order to guarantee that technology is used as a tool for society advancement rather than as a cause of injustice or disruption, this three-way cooperation is essential.

There are a lot of potential and difficult problems associated with incorporating Living Intelligence into workforce development, education, and social institutions. By tailoring instruction and offering real-time feedback, adaptive learning systems and AI tutoring platforms have the potential to revolutionize education and make it more effective and entertaining. In the meanwhile, to prosper in a convergent tech landscape, the changing workforce needs to be reskilled and given new skills. However, social effects from better quality of life to possible injustices need to be carefully managed by ethical governance and effective public policy.

To guarantee that these revolutionary technologies are applied responsibly, strong regulatory frameworks created via cooperation between the public and private sectors are crucial. The objective is to protect individual rights and advance social justice while utilizing Living Intelligence's potential to stimulate innovation and advancement.

Looking ahead, it is certain that the combination of biotechnology, sensor technology, and artificial intelligence will transform not only how we work and learn, but also the structure of society as a whole. The obstacles are numerous, but with careful preparation, ongoing adaptation, and cooperative governance, we can create the conditions for a day when technology improves all facets of life in a way that is morally just, sustainable, and inclusive.

CHAPTER 9

EMERGING TECHNOLOGIES AND FUTURE TRENDS

The merger of several cutting-edge sectors and quick invention will define technology in the future. Looking ahead, a number of significant phenomena hold the potential to change sectors, reinterpret intelligence, and alter how we engage with the outside world. In addition to providing forecasts for the upcoming decade of convergence that will propel the development of Living Intelligence, this chapter explores new developments in artificial intelligence, synthetic biology, sensor fusion, and decentralized computing.

9.1 AI and Cognitive Systems of the Future

Research on next-generation AI is set to expand the capabilities of intelligent systems. According to emerging trends, AI in the future will be distinguished by systems that more closely resemble human cognition in addition to having more potent computational models.

1. Future Directions for AI Research and Development:

XAI (Explainable AI):

The goal of research is to create interpretable and transparent AI models. Understanding how and why judgments are produced is crucial for stakeholders as AI systems are being included into decision-making processes in crucial industries like healthcare and finance.

Bullet Points:

- Enhanced adoption and trust in industries subject to regulations.
- Bias is lessened, and accountability is enhanced.

Multimodal Education:

Models that can combine information from several sources, including as text, images, audio, and sensory inputs, to create a deeper comprehension of intricate situations are the key to the future of artificial intelligence. For example, these multimodal systems can provide more context-aware responses by combining natural language processing with visual input.

Bullet Points:

- Increased awareness of context.
- Better performance in practical applications.

Decision-Making on its Own:

Systems that can make judgments on their own in addition to analyzing data are becoming more and more common. This tendency is especially noticeable in fields where real-time processing and adaptive decision-making are essential, including robotics and driverless cars.

Complementing Edge Computing:

The requirement to process data closer to the source is growing as AI systems get more complex. By processing computation locally rather than only depending on centralized data centers, edge computing enables AI to function with reduced latency and enhanced privacy.

2. Quantum computing and neuromorphic architectures' implications:

The concept of quantum computing

By resolving issues that are computationally unsolvable for traditional computers, quantum computing holds the potential to completely transform artificial intelligence. Its capacity to handle massive volumes of data concurrently may result in advances in modeling, pattern recognition, and optimization.

Bullet Points:

- Significant speedup in the training of intricate models.
- Improved capacity for handling massive data sets.
- The capacity to effectively resolve combinatorial optimization issues.

As an example, neuromorphic architectures

Neuromorphic computing creates chips that mimic neural architecture, drawing inspiration from the human brain. The goal of these systems is to increase processing speed and energy efficiency in tasks involving perception and sensory integration.

Bullet Points:

- Power consumption is lower than with conventional GPUs.

- Better results when performing activities that call for quick decisions.

- Encouraging more human-like flexibility and learning.

In conclusion, trends emphasizing transparency, integrating various data sources, and autonomous decision-making will influence the landscape of next-generation AI. Particularly, quantum computing and neuromorphic architectures hold promise for breaking new ground in AI efficiency and performance, opening the door to more potent and human-centered systems.

9.2 The Prospects of Living Machines and Synthetic Biology

The distinction between biological systems and constructed devices is becoming increasingly hazy in the fast developing field of synthetic biology. By combining the accuracy and scalability of built systems, this convergence promises to produce "living machines" that are capable of carrying out activities that have historically been performed by biological beings.

1. New Developments in Synthetic Biology:

Creating Innovative Organisms:

Scientists may create new living entities from the ground up thanks to synthetic biology. Scientists can design creatures with certain functions by using standardized genetic components. For instance, microorganisms that have been modified may be able to break down environmental contaminants or create biofuels.

Systems Biomimetic:

Systems that imitate biological processes have been developed as a result of advancements in this discipline. Biohybrid robots, tissue scaffolds, and artificial cells are early instances of the intersection of materials science, robotics, and synthetic biology.

Bullet Points:

- Personalized cells for precise medication administration.

- Biohybrid robots that are capable of self-healing and adaptation.
- Regenerative medicine using engineered tissues.

Digital Platform Integration:

Synthetic biology is largely driven by developments in computational biology and bioinformatics. Rapid creation and testing of synthetic structures is made possible by computers' capacity to model and simulate intricate biological processes.

2. Experimental Prototypes and New Applications:

Life-giving machines:

The potential of synthetic biology is demonstrated by experimental prototypes such biohybrid robots that blend synthetic and organic materials or create bacteria that make medications. These systems can function in conditions that are difficult for traditional machinery to handle.

Applications in the Environment:

There is potential for using synthetic biology to solve environmental issues. A more sustainable future can be achieved by engineering organisms to absorb carbon, clean up oil spills, or turn trash into usable products.

Applications in Medicine:

While genetically modified organisms present new avenues for customized therapy, the creation of artificial tissues and organs has the potential to transform transplant medicine.

The following are bullet points for applications:

- Bioengineered cells for targeted medication administration.
- Synthetic tissues for the regeneration of organs.
- Microbes that have been engineered to clean up the environment.
- Biomimetic sensors to assess health in real time.

What we think of as "living machines" will be redefined by the confluence of synthetic biology, digital tools, and artificial intelligence. These systems have the capacity to carry out intricate, adaptive tasks that conventional machines are unable to, thereby bridging the gap between the biological and the artificial.

9.3 Developments in Edge Computing and Sensor Fusion

Two essential technologies that allow for real-time analytics and decision-making at the point of data production are sensor fusion and edge computing. The capacity to effectively integrate and interpret this data is crucial for responsive and adaptive systems as sensor networks proliferate.

1. Decentralized Data Processing Trends:

Methods of Sensor Fusion:

By merging data from several sensors, sensor fusion creates information that is more precise, thorough, and trustworthy than that which could be gleaned from using only one sensor. There are various levels at which this integration might happen:

Feature-Level Fusion: Combining unprocessed data from several sources to create a single dataset.

- To reach an agreement, the outputs of many sensor

systems are combined in a process known as "Decision-Level Fusion."

Hybrid Approaches: combining the two techniques to increase precision and robustness.

Insights in Real Time:

The proliferation of sensor data makes real-time processing essential. Faster reaction times and less strain on centralized data centers are made possible by decentralized processing.

2. How Edge Computing Helps Make Responsive Systems Possible:

Processing at the Boundaries:

Instead of sending data to a central cloud, edge computing processes data close to the source. This reduces latency, improves privacy, and enables real-time decision-making, all of which are essential for applications like industrial automation and driverless cars.

Cost Savings and Energy Efficiency:

Edge computing can drastically reduce energy usage and

operating expenses by eliminating the requirement for continuous data transfer.

Highlights of the Advantages of Edge Computing:

- Reduced latency and quicker reaction times.
- Improved privacy and security of data.
- Energy and bandwidth requirements have decreased.
- Scalability for extensive networks of sensors.

3. Combining Edge Computing with Sensor Fusion:

Systems that are responsive and able to adjust to changing environments are produced by combining sensor fusion techniques with edge computing. For instance:

Applications for Smart Cities:

Traffic lights and pollution control measures can be instantly adjusted thanks to edge devices' local processing of data from environmental monitors and traffic sensors.

Automation in Industry:

Edge computer units in a manufacturing facility can combine information from temperature, pressure, and vibration sensors to forecast equipment problems and initiate automated maintenance procedures.

Healthcare Surveillance:

Multiple sensor-equipped wearables can interpret biometric data locally, giving users immediate feedback and warning medical personnel of emergencies.

Building adaptable, resilient, and intelligent systems requires sensor fusion and edge computing, which enable decentralized, real-time analytics. These technologies guarantee that information gathered from numerous sources is promptly converted into useful insights, increasing productivity and enhancing decision-making in a variety of fields.

9.4 Projecting the Upcoming Convergence Decade

In the future, there will likely be a significant change in the market dynamics and disruptive breakthroughs as a result of the acceleration of the convergence of AI, biotechnology, and sensor technologies. The upcoming ten years are expected to bring about revolutionary shifts that will reshape our interactions with technology and our surroundings.

1. Models and Forecasts for the Development of Living Intelligence:

Convergence of Emergence:

The distinctions between biological and digital systems should become increasingly hazy as integration gets more smooth. The idea of emergence where new, unanticipated traits evolve from the complex interactions of integrated systems is frequently central to models that forecast this evolution.

Multimodal Intelligence's Growth:

In order to provide more complex insights and responses, systems will be able to process and integrate a wider variety of input kinds, including visual, aural, genetic, and environmental data. Applications that are more context-aware and tailored will be made possible by this development.

The following are bullet points for future predictions:

- Increased adaptability and autonomy in

interconnected systems.

- A greater dependence on localized, real-time data processing.

- Improved cooperation between synthetic and biological elements.

- A move toward systems that proactively anticipate changes rather than just responding to them.

2. Potential Market Shifts and Disruptive Innovations:

Healthcare Revolution:

Significant advances in personalized medicine will result from the confluence of AI, real-time biosensing, and genetic profiling, allowing for the development of therapies that are specific to each patient's genetic and physiological characteristics. This change has the potential to upend established healthcare structures and spur the creation of fresh, more effective treatment regimens.

Sustainable Urban Living and Smart Cities:

Urban surroundings will become more efficient and adaptable with improved sensor networks and edge computing. Initiatives for smart cities will improve public services, save energy costs, and enhance people's quality of life in general. Both public and private investments are anticipated to propel the smart infrastructure market's exponential growth.

Making and Automation in Industry:

Manufacturing processes will continue to be revolutionized by the integration of sensor fusion with AI-driven analytics. Adaptive manufacturing lines, real-time quality control, and predictive maintenance will become commonplace, reducing expenses and boosting operational effectiveness.

Impacts on the Economy and Society:

These technologies' quick development could cause major changes in the work sector, requiring extensive retraining and adaptation. Furthermore, the democratization of cutting-edge technologies raises concerns about access and equity but may help lessen gaps between established and emerging nations.

3. Next Decade Strategic Roadmap:

Investments in Research and Development:

R&D expenditures must be sustained. To finance interdisciplinary research that examines the integration of AI, biotech, and sensing technologies, governments, businesses, and academic institutions must work together.

Adaptation to Regulation and Ethics:

Regulations must change to meet new issues as these converging technologies develop. To guarantee that innovation occurs ethically, standards for data protection, moral AI application, and the fusion of digital and biological systems must be established.

Workforce Transition and Market Adaptation:

Convergence will bring about disruptive changes that industries will need to adjust to. To stay competitive, this entails investing in personnel reskilling, modernizing company models, and cultivating an atmosphere of constant innovation.

The strategic roadmap's bullet points are as follows:

- Funding for transdisciplinary R&D has increased.
- The creation of adaptable and flexible regulatory

systems.

- Funding for reskilling and worker education initiatives.
- Promoting collaborations between the public and private sectors to stimulate innovation and commercialization.

4. The long-term outlook for living intelligence is as follows:

Living Intelligence will undergo significant change in the future. In the upcoming ten years, we can expect that:

Systems will start to evolve on their own:

In addition to learning and adapting in real time, integrated systems may also start to evolve on their own by absorbing fresh information and user input.

Our world will be defined by interconnectedness:

When digital and biological systems are seamlessly integrated, hyper-connected environments will result, with intelligent communication and collaboration between all of the components, from personal devices to metropolitan infrastructure.

The phenomenon of human-machine symbiosis

A new era of symbiosis, in which technology augments human talents rather than completely replaces them, will arise as the lines between human and machine intelligence continue to blur.

Long-Term Vision Bullet Points:

- Systems have evolved from reactive to anticipatory.
- Enhanced cooperation between artificial and organic intelligence.
- Pervasive interconnectedness in the urban, industrial, and personal spheres.
- A move toward integrated, comprehensive systems that reinterpret daily existence.

The convergence of AI, biotechnology, and sensing technologies is expected to bring about an unparalleled shift in the upcoming ten years. With the help of quantum computing and neuromorphic architectures, next-generation AI systems will bring about a new era of cognitive computing that is more transparent, adaptive, and focused on people. The boundaries between the biological and the artificial will continue to blur as a result of advancements in synthetic biology, creating living devices that may be used for everything from environmental remediation to personalized medicine.

Our capacity to process and respond to real-time data will be further improved by developments in sensor fusion and edge computing, resulting in responsive and adaptable systems. Smart cities, sophisticated industrial automation, and more effective resource management will all be made possible by this decentralized approach to data processing, which will be essential for handling the massive volumes of data produced by linked devices.

Predicting the future of living intelligence entails not just anticipating new developments in technology but also comprehending the wider social, economic, and regulatory changes that will coincide with these breakthroughs. The equitable and sustainable realization of these advantages will require deliberate investments in R&D, workforce development, and ethical governance as disruptive technologies transform industries and open up new markets.

All facets of our life could be revolutionized by the merging of these disparate technologies. It will result in more intelligent, flexible settings where systems can adapt to new problems and decisions are based on real-time data. Government, business, and academic cooperation will be essential as we traverse this revolutionary terrain in order to create a future that is not just technologically sophisticated but also morally sound and inclusive of everyone.

We may use Living Intelligence to build a more resilient, effective, and responsive world that meets the needs of people and society as a whole by comprehending and planning for these emerging trends.

CHAPTER 10

DIFFICULTIES, HAZARDS, AND MANAGEMENT

There is a great deal of potential for societal change due to the quick development and convergence of technology in the field of living intelligence. But enormous power also carries a great deal of responsibility. We face a number of hazards and concerns as we incorporate biotechnology, AI, and sensor technologies into systems that affect every part of our life. These problems range from moral conundrums and privacy issues to the dangers of excessive dependency and negative social effects. Furthermore, to guarantee that innovation proceeds responsibly, it is imperative to establish strong governance models and regulatory frameworks. We examine the difficulties, dangers, and governance issues related to living intelligence in detail in this chapter, and we offer solutions for responsible innovation and mitigation.

10.1 Privacy and Ethical Issues in Living Intelligence

By definition, living intelligence systems are made to gather, process, and evaluate enormous volumes of environmental and personal data. Protecting individual rights and society values requires addressing significant ethical conundrums and privacy concerns brought up by this data-driven approach.

1. Converged Technologies' Ethical Conundrums:

Decision-Making and Autonomy:

AI systems frequently take on tasks that were previously only performed by human decision-makers when they are combined with biotechnology and sensor networks. The degree to which machines should be trusted to make important decisions is called into question by this change. AI-driven diagnostic tools in the healthcare industry, for example, may recommend treatment regimens that have a big impact on patient outcomes.

- How much autonomy is appropriate for machines?
- In the event that an AI-driven decision causes harm,

how should responsibility be allocated?

The concept of bias and fairness

The possibility that AI systems will pick up and reinforce prejudices from the data they are trained on raises further ethical questions. These prejudices have the potential to exacerbate already-existing societal injustices by resulting in disparate treatment of various populations.

- How may bias be reduced in system design?
- What safeguards ought to be in place to guarantee equity in automated decision-making?

Transparency and Consent:

Making sure people are aware of how their data is used becomes crucial in an ecosystem where data is continuously gathered and examined. In order for people to comprehend the ramifications of data sharing, consent must be acquired in a transparent and thorough manner.

2. Data Privacy and Possible Personal Information Misuse:

Collecting Sensitive Data:

Sensitive personal data is frequently handled by living intelligence systems, ranging from genetic data utilized in tailored medicine to biometric data collected by wearable sensors. One major worry is the possibility of this data being misused. Identity theft, discrimination, or even deliberate manipulation may result from unauthorized access or data breaches.

Data protection and anonymity:

Strong anonymization procedures must be put in place in order to safeguard individual identities. This calls for methods like stringent access controls, secure transmission routes, and data encryption.

Bullet Points:

- Encrypting sensitive data from beginning to end.
- Regular security checks and safe data storage.
- Strict access controls and multi-factor authentication are being implemented.

Conscientious Consent:

People need to know exactly what information is being gathered, how it will be used, and who will have access to it. Users should have the freedom to choose whether or not to participate in this process, and it should be transparent.

Stakeholders may create systems that promote technology innovation while simultaneously upholding the principles of justice, openness, and respect for individual liberty by tackling these ethical and privacy issues.

10.2 The Dangers of Technological Disruption and Overdependence

Significant gains may result from the integration of Living Intelligence systems, but an excessive reliance on technology is also a risk. Rapid adoption without sufficient protections can result in vulnerabilities that affect people's livelihoods and society as a whole.

1. Overdependence Scenarios:

Systemic vulnerabilities include:
Any failure, whether brought on by technical issues, cyberattacks, or simply basic human error, can have a domino effect because cities, healthcare systems, and

industrial processes are becoming more and more dependent on automated, networked systems. For example, a broad failure in the sensor network of a smart city might simultaneously affect public safety, energy distribution, and traffic control systems.

Relocation of Work:

AI-driven procedures and automation have the potential to replace occupations, particularly those involving routine or repeated tasks. Even while there will be new opportunities, if the transition period is not handled well, it could cause serious economic upheaval and more unemployment.

Over-reliance and social isolation:

Social repercussions may also result from an over reliance on technology. Social isolation and a deterioration of community ties may result from people depending too much on digital interfaces for communication and decision-making at the expense of in-person encounters.

Bullet Points on Overdependence Risks:

- System-wide malfunctions brought on by technical issues.

- Disruption of the economy due to employment displacement.
- A higher susceptibility to cyberattacks.
- A decrease in interpersonal connections and social isolation.

2. Technological Upheaval and Backup Plans:

Strong risk management and backup plans are necessary to mitigate the hazards brought on by the quick adoption of new technologies.

Frameworks for Assessing Risk:

Businesses need to evaluate the risks associated with their reliance on technology on a frequent basis. Assessing their infrastructure's resilience, data security, and cascading failure risk are all part of this.

Fail-safes and redundancy:

The impact of a system failure can be lessened by putting fail-safes and redundant mechanisms in place. For instance, backup systems that can smoothly take over in the case of an interruption should be installed for vital infrastructure, such as transportation networks and electricity grids.

Plans for Disaster Recovery:

It is crucial to have thorough disaster recovery plans that cover procedures for technical failures, natural disasters, and cyberattacks. To make sure these strategies continue to work in changing circumstances, they should be tested and updated on a regular basis.

Through proactive risk management, stakeholders may create robust systems that can withstand the demands of swift technology advancements.

10.3 Governance Models and Regulatory Frameworks

Strong governance models and legal frameworks are necessary to guarantee that technological breakthroughs benefit all stakeholders while reducing dangers, especially in light of the significant impact that living intelligence has on society.

1. Examining Current Regulatory Environments:

Present-day Frameworks:

Numerous jurisdictions have enacted laws pertaining to privacy and data protection, such as the Health Insurance Portability and Accountability Act (HIPAA) in the US and the General Data Protection Regulation (GDPR) in Europe. These frameworks offer a starting point for safeguarding private information and guaranteeing responsibility.

Finding the Gaps:

However, because modern technologies are convergent, current restrictions frequently fall short. Traditional rules do not fully address the particular issues created by the integration of biotechnology, sensor networks, and artificial intelligence.

Bullet Points:

- The absence of thorough rules for data gathered by networked systems.
- AI-driven decision-making is not adequately regulated.
- The ethical ramifications of convergent technologies are not adequately addressed.

2. Offering Models of Governance:

The concept of collaborative governance

Collaboration amongst a variety of stakeholders, including governments, business executives, academic institutions, and civil society organizations, is necessary for the effective governance of living intelligence. Models of collaborative governance encourage openness, responsibility, and accountability.

Frameworks for Adaptive Regulation:

For regulatory frameworks to stay up with technological changes, they must be adaptable and agile. Establishing regulatory sandboxes where novel technologies can be evaluated in controlled settings prior to broad adoption may be one way to achieve this.

Ethical Standards and Guidelines:

It is essential to create ethical standards that cover topics like accountability, bias, and fairness. Experts from a variety of disciplines should be consulted when creating these recommendations, and they should be evaluated on a regular basis as technology advances.

The following are bullet points about governance models:

- Frameworks for collaboration with several parties.
- Flexible and adaptive regulatory systems.
- The creation of moral guidelines for new technologies.
- To guarantee ongoing relevance, there should be regular reviews and updates.

3. An example of a case:

A multi-stakeholder advisory board of representatives from digital businesses, urban planning organizations, privacy advocates, and academic experts may be established by a government enacting new regulations for smart cities. This board would supervise the implementation of sensor networks and AI systems, guaranteeing responsible data collection, privacy protection, and adherence to ethical standards. An approach like this encourages openness and increases public confidence in the application of cutting-edge technologies.

10.4 Mitigation and Responsible Innovation Techniques

Proactive approaches that promote ethical innovation while reducing potential drawbacks are necessary to address the dangers and problems related to living intelligence.

1. Industry Stakeholders' Best Practices:

Strong Security Procedures:

Modern cybersecurity techniques must be used by industry participants to safeguard data and guarantee the robustness of networked systems. This comprises:

- Frequent penetration tests and security audits.
- Encrypting data both in transit and at rest from beginning to end.
- Strict identity management and access control.

Accountability and Transparency:

Businesses ought to implement procedures that encourage openness in their business dealings. Data regarding system performance, security lapses, and repair initiatives may be published as part of this. Mechanisms for accountability, such certification procedures and third-party audits, can increase trust even more.

Ongoing Education and Retraining:

The personnel must change along with the technology. Putting money into ongoing training initiatives guarantees that staff members have the know-how to properly manage and operate sophisticated technology.

The following are bullet points regarding industry best practices:

- The application of state-of-the-art cybersecurity techniques.
- Structures for accountability and reporting that are transparent.
- Frequent skill development and training initiatives for staff members.
- Adoption of certificates and industry standards.

2. Governments, Industry, and Academics Working Together:

Because of the intricacy of the problems presented by living intelligence, cooperation is required:

PPPs, or public-private partnerships, are:

Governments can establish public-private partnerships that

foster innovation while guaranteeing regulatory compliance and the general welfare by collaborating with academic institutions and business leaders.

Consortia for Research and Innovation:

Consortia that bring together specialists from different disciplines can promote interdisciplinary research and hasten the creation of solutions that tackle ethical and technical problems.

Policy Discussions and Workshops:

Frequent discussions among academic experts, industry leaders, and legislators can aid in the development of flexible and responsive regulatory frameworks. Conferences and workshops offer forums for exchanging cutting-edge ideas and best practices.

The following are bullet points on collaborative strategies:

- The establishment of public-private partnerships for collaborative innovation initiatives.
- Consortia for interdisciplinary research are established.

- Frequent policy discussions to modernize and improve regulatory structures.

- Involvement with civil society to guarantee that public interests are reflected in policies.

3. Creating a Responsible Innovation Roadmap:

A strategic roadmap for responsible innovation entails establishing precise goals and success indicators.

Frameworks for Risk Management:

Comprehensive risk management frameworks that pinpoint any weaknesses, evaluate their consequences, and lay out backup plans should be created by organizations. It is important to regularly examine and update these frameworks to take into account emerging issues.

Rewards for Moral Behavior:

Companies that follow moral principles and put strong data protection safeguards in place can receive incentives from governments and regulatory agencies. Tax breaks, grants, or public recognition are a few examples of this.

Observation and Assessment:

It is crucial to continuously monitor the implementation of technology. Systems function as planned and risks are immediately handled with the support of independent audits, performance reviews, and feedback systems.

The Responsible Innovation Roadmap's bullet points are as follows:

- The creation of all-encompassing risk management plans.
- Encouragement of moral behavior with government assistance.
- Constant observation, assessment, and impartial audits.
- Clearly defined measures and standards for innovation success.

In conclusion, there are a number of risks and difficulties associated with the fusion of biotechnology, AI, and sensor technologies into Living Intelligence that need to be properly addressed. Careful consideration must be given to the risks of society upheaval, over-reliance on technology, and ethical and privacy issues. To guarantee that new technologies are applied responsibly and fairly, strong governance models and regulatory frameworks created through cooperation between the public and private sectors are crucial.

In addition to implementing best practices, like strong security procedures, openness initiatives, and ongoing employee training, strategies for mitigation and responsible innovation also entail creating cooperative frameworks that unite various parties. Society can take advantage of Living Intelligence's enormous potential while avoiding its drawbacks by putting in place flexible regulatory frameworks, rewarding moral conduct, and developing well-defined risk management plans.

The problems presented by living intelligence are intricate and multidimensional as we look to the future. But we can overcome these obstacles and clear the path for a day when technology advancement improves human lives in a way that is safe, just, and sustainable if we plan ahead, collaborate across disciplines, and remain steadfastly committed to moral values. Responsible innovation is a continuous process, but by tackling these issues head-on, we can build a future where technology promotes wealth and advancement while maintaining the principles that make up our society.

ABOUT THE AUTHOR

Author and thought leader in the IT field Taylor Royce is well known. He has a two-decade career and is an expert at tech trend analysis and forecasting, which enables a wide audience to understand complicated concepts.

Royce's considerable involvement in the IT industry stemmed from his passion with technology, which he developed during his computer science studies. He has extensive knowledge of the industry because of his experience in both software development and strategic consulting.

Known for his research and lucidity, he has written multiple best-selling books and contributed to esteemed tech periodicals. Translations of Royce's books throughout the world demonstrate his impact.

Royce is a well-known authority on emerging technologies and their effects on society, frequently requested as a speaker at international conferences and as a guest on tech podcasts. He promotes the development of ethical technology, emphasizing problems like data privacy and the digital divide.

In addition, with a focus on sustainable industry growth, Royce mentors upcoming tech experts and supports IT education projects. Taylor Royce is well known for his ability to combine analytical thinking with technical know-how. He sees a time when technology will ethically benefit humanity.

www.ingramcontent.com/pod-product-compliance
Lightning Source LLC
LaVergne TN
LVHW022345060326
832902LV00022B/4245